TOWN&COUNTRY

MANNERS &
MISDEMEANORS

Notes on POST-CIVILIZED Society

Edited by Ash Carter

HEARST
books

HEARSTBOOKS

An Imprint of Sterling Publishing Co., Inc.
1166 Avenue of the Americas
New York, NY 10036

Town & Country is a registered trademark of
Hearst Communications, Inc.

© 2016 by Hearst Communications, Inc.

"SENSITIVITY"
Words by MARSHALL BARER. Music by MARY RODGERS.
©1959 (Renewed) CHAPPELL & CO., INC.
All rights reserved. Used by permission of ALFRED MUSIC.

ISBN 978-1-61837-221-5

Distributed in Canada by Sterling Publishing Co., Inc.
c/o Canadian Manda Group, 664 Annette Street
Toronto, Ontario, Canada M6S 2C8
Distributed in the United Kingdom by GMC Distribution Services
Castle Place, 166 High Street, Lewes, East Sussex, England BN7 1XU
Distributed in Australia by NewSouth Books
45 Beach Street, Coogee, NSW 2034, Australia

For information about custom editions, special sales, and premium
and corporate purchases, please contact Sterling Special Sales at
800-805-5489 or specialsales@sterlingpublishing.com.

Manufactured in the United States of America

2 4 6 8 10 9 7 5 3 1

www.sterlingpublishing.com

Design by Philip Buchanan
Cover and interior illustrations by Edwin Fotheringham

CONTENTS

A NOTE FROM THE EDITORS

As Cleveland Amory once noted, "to say that present-day Society is just fine, great shape, wonderful people, etc., is tantamount to an admission that one has never known better . . . One is obviously open to the charge of being newly arrived."

And *Town & Country*—which turns 170 this year—was already three quarters of a century old by the time that parvenu Emily Post appeared on the scene.

The column from which most of the essays in this book were pulled was introduced twenty-one years ago "to address the erosion of decorum" that the editors had begun to notice all around them. "It was time for *Town & Country* to throw down the gauntlet." But *T&C* had thrown down the gauntlet before. In fact, the gauntlet was pretty dinged-up.

As far back as 1900, another concerned citizen (a lady named Amelia Gere Mason) was cautioning the magazine's readers that "there is nothing more contagious than bad manners," lamenting that "the rush and hurry of life in which everybody is intent upon doing the most in the least possible time" left no "time for small courtesies . . . Manners are being trampled out in the mad march of something we call progress."

Manners, it seems, are a little like spotted owls: often written about, seldom observed. The following pieces were composed accordingly, not under the illusion that human decency once flourished, but in the hope that it doesn't go completely extinct.

This book will not teach you how to set a table, or what kind of flowers to send, or the meaning of "festive attire." When Jay Fielden assumed the editorship five years ago, he felt that such topics were belabored—and had been since the Kennedy administration. Instead, he sought field notes from those areas where shifting ground had unsettled the social order, ruffling the spotted owls.

The resulting dispatches, the best of which are collected here, cover subjects you won't find addressed in the existing literature, from the unwritten laws of kindergarten admissions to the new sport of competitive dining to contemporary art that makes the *avant-garde* blush to the proliferating configurations of the American family.

It is our hope that the contributors anthologized herein exhibit "that higher class of intelligence"— Frau Mason again—"which sees things not only as they are, but as they ought to be." At the very least, no one can call them *nouveau*.

Chapter 1

FOOD

THE HUNGER GAMES

BY BOB MORRIS

WELCOME TO THE PUNISHING NEW WORLD
OF COMPETITION DINING, WHERE THE AGONY
OF GETTING A RESERVATION ONLY MAKES
YOUR MEAL TASTE BETTER.

I t's nine p.m. sharp in a grim working-class neighborhood outside Girona, Spain, and the foodies are descending on El Celler de Can Roca. Many step out of cabs coming from the train station or from downtown hotels in the small inland city, an hour or so north of Barcelona. They pose for one another in the glare of an illuminated sign. They look anticipatory and self-congratulatory. Well, who can blame them?

El Celler de Can Roca is often described as Catalonia's successor to Ferran Adrià's El Bulli, which reigned until 2011 outside Roses, another small city nearby. But although it has appeared on every list of best restaurants for years and has the highest Michelin rank of three stars, and even though it beat Copenhagen's Noma in 2013 as *Restaurant* magazine's number one restaurant in the world, El Celler de Can Roca is not exactly a household name. Unless you live in the house of restaurant fanaticism.

I don't. But that doesn't mean I'm not as susceptible to suggestion as the next competitive traveler. When I told friends I would be in Catalonia in October, they told me where I had to have my trophy dinner. It usually takes a year to get a table, but with the magic of publishing connections and persistent e-mailing, I scared up a place sooner than that. The satisfaction I felt watching faces change when I told people about my reservation reminded me of telling young mothers that my little niece had gotten into a top school on the Upper East Side. The odds of getting into El Celler de Can Roca are about the same.

After a long, circuitous drive, my companion and I step past walls of ivy into the garden of a turn-of-the-century villa connected to an adamantly modern addition. Inside a futuristic white interior, a kitchen door opens and closes for the swiftly moving staff (the restaurant has a ratio of about one employee to each guest, better than the faculty-to-student ratio at Williams) with a pneumatic *whoosh* that's very starship *Enterprise*. We choose the fourteen-course tasting dinner with wine pairings, for about 300 euros each. The price seems modest given not just the meal but the elevated status it offers among the indoctrinated.

AH, THE PLEASURES OF DINING OUT ON DINING out! at a time when just about everything we do seems to be either for presentational display on social media or an occasion for one-upmanship, who can resist the siren call of the costly and geographically challenging three-star Michelin meal?

Ask anyone in the know, and he'll have a pilgrim's tale of his *hajj* to an important foodie mecca, from the French Laundry in Napa to Combal.Zero in Piedmont, Italy. In 2010, Eric Ripert, the celebrity chef at Le Bernardin, took a day off to fly from New York to Spain and back just to eat dinner at El Bulli. "It wasn't my style of cooking, but it was intense," he tells me. Kate Krader, the restaurant editor of

Food & Wine, made the journey to Fäviken, hours from Stockholm. "It was a trip with trains, boats, and planes, and it was totally worth the trouble," she says.

Then there's Bonjwing Lee, the self-dubbed "gastronaut" behind the Ulterior Epicure website, which is for extreme foodies. In 2005, while a law student in Holland, he became obsessed with a three-star Michelin restaurant, L'Arnsbourg, high in the Vosges Mountains of Lorraine. He arrived at a godforsaken rural train station before dawn one winter morning with a bike he had rented, because the cab fare to the restaurant would have cost more than the lunch. He had five hours to kill and nowhere to keep warm. So, after being taken in by a baker and his wife (he helped them make bûches de Noël), he rode fifteen kilometers in freezing cold, and upon his arrival for lunch in a ski parka and hat, he asked the hostess if he could use the restroom to change into the suit and tie in his backpack. "She asked if I needed a doctor instead," said the clearly frigid Lee, who has organized squadrons of friends to call simultaneously at the moment reservation lines open at top restaurants around the world. "But I was fine, and I had the most wonderful lunch." The ride back to the train station in the dark was partly uphill. But he made it.

Given that the Michelin system suggests that three stars is "worth a journey," it's no wonder in this conspicuous consumerist culture that travelers plan entire trips around a meal. But for all the happy tales on foodie trails, there are occasional skid marks and mishaps. These include an outbreak of diarrhea and vomiting among 60 guests at Noma in 2013 (the year it lost its number-one spot to El Celler de Can Roca) and something similar with larger numbers at Fat Duck in rural England, which was rated the world's best restaurant in 2005.

Sometimes the travel itself can be sickening. My brother and sister-in-law once spent three hours in a cab with a non–English-speaking driver who couldn't find El Celler de Can Roca. One New York psychologist told me that because of high winds a cruise ship that was supposed to get him to Copenhagen in time for his Noma reservation was delayed. He missed his dinner, but he consoled himself with knowing he would not have to eat the ants on the menu. Jodie Foster, who had been told she had to wait two years for a Noma reservation (socialist-leaning countries do not break rules for celebrities), got a similar last-minute availability call (for lunch) and dropped everything to go. And after a high-powered friend of mine in public relations waited with her father in the cold for hours to eat at Barcelona's top tapas place, Tapas 24, which is tiny and run by an Adrià disciple, they became sick, joining the ranks of other three-star global gourmands. The same friend has also shown up to beg at Lebrina in Tasmania. "I told them I had come all the way from Manhattan, and they thought I was insane," she says.

In a recent *New Yorker* essay the British food writer John Lanchester suggested that, while food used to be about where you came from, it's now about where you want to go and who you want to be. And so, for the adamantly aspirational, that means, of course, where you can't get in.

For those who won't take no, Nobu's Drew Nieporent, whose Bâtard earned its first Michelin star recently, doesn't recommend gaming the system by booking five p.m. tables you don't intend to use. Instead, he says, be honest. "The point is we have to fill seats, so if you're nice we'll be nice," he says. Louise Vongerichten, daughter of Jean-Georges, agrees. "You don't have to say you know my dad," she says. "I like to know you tried getting a table on your own before I step in to help." Ripert has another suggestion. "I tell people to call my wife," he says. "She knows more about reservations at the restaurant than I do, and she doesn't even work there!"

One thing is certain: When you're in, you're in, and that means anything goes. At El Celler de Can Roca, where the three Roca brothers are treated like rock stars, an infatuated diner asked Joan Roca, the main chef, to sign her breast with a marker. Others scream or burst into tears on seeing sexy Jordi Roca, whom Michelin ranks the world's best pastry chef. Some diners sleep in the garden and ask to be woken up for the first train back to Barcelona. (There are toothbrushes for them in the sleek bathrooms.) As for me, I chuck etiquette aside and take pictures of each dish. Nobody on the staff raises an eyebrow—but, then, we're in Spain, not France. And the table is ours for the night, because there's only one seating.

We have the famous caramelized olives on a bonsai tree to start, and then applaud as waiters open paper globes to showcase five morsels of intense flavors inspired by international dishes. "We present to you the world," one announces. There's even a sourdough ice cream with dried lychee and Jerez vinegar meringue served on a battery-operated pulsating blob sculpture "to celebrate fermentation," we are told, and perhaps, we also have to assume, local surrealist Salvador Dalí.

Nothing isn't delicious, visually stunning, and provocative. "Society needs something new," Josef Roca, the restaurant's wine expert, tells us after dinner, at one in the morning.

Society also needs something to go home and brag about. I have been doing so ever since.

TABLE TROUBLE

BY DWIGHT GARNER

DINING OUT OR ORDERING IN, NOBODY
SEEMS TO CARE ABOUT THE FINER POINTS
OF EATING—OR SERVING—ANYMORE.
IT'S TIME TO PUT A FORK IN IT.

T he loveliest dining scene in the history of
American film is to be found not in one of those
movies that hungry people like to watch and
rewatch—*Big Night*, *Sideways*, *Ratatouille*—but in
the sly and sophisticated 1963 Stanley Donen film
Charade, with Audrey Hepburn and Cary Grant.
The scene lasts only a few moments. Don't refill your
wineglass without pausing; you might miss it.

Hepburn and Grant are dining on a boat on the
Seine, their crisp repartee echoing off the stone

arches of the bridges they pass beneath. She's a widow threatened by men who are after her late husband's possibly stolen money; he's a charming chameleon who may only want her money, too. The movie slows to a crawl when Hepburn delicately picks up her fork in her left hand, tines down, and her spoon in her right, curved gently upward, and begins to compose a salad from a serving dish. She flicks lettuce and charcuterie onto her salad plate with an adroitness and ease that are nearly supernatural. This, one thinks, is what the proper use of cutlery looks like. Her posture and manners are almost heartbreaking to observe.

They definitely break Cary Grant's heart. Watching her, he finally utters what's been on his mind all along. "Hasn't it occurred to you," he says, "that I'm having a hard time keeping my hands off you?" She melts, and after a few seconds her cutlery crashes to the table. One kind of spell has been broken; another kind has been cast.

I've had Audrey Hepburn and *Charade* on my mind recently while eating out, often downheartedly, in New York City and elsewhere. I've been thinking about how rare lovely table manners have become, and how they've combined with dismal service in restaurants—these two things have a profound impact on each other—to create an era-defining feedback loop of discourteousness and clatter. It's enough to make you want to, in a variation on Hannibal Lecter's favorite cocktail, mix a martini from your own tears.

It hurts the eyes to look around in restaurants. Napkins aren't in laps; cell phones and keys are out on tables; forks are clutched like screwdrivers; talking mouths are stuffed, like soft tacos, with food. Manners can seem, in all but the most elite of restaurants, to have gone underground, like a gene that has skipped a generation. I used to mourn that restaurant lighting had grown so dim. I like to see what I'm eating. Now I worship the gloom. The candlelight hides the chaos, in addition to fulfilling its traditional and more blissful purpose: that of making women look even more beautiful.

It's easy to sound like a ninny for noticing what's going on. We're living in an unpretentious, informal, well-tattooed restaurant moment, and here's a hearty toast to all of that. (I agree with Napoleon, who said, "In victory you deserve champagne. In defeat you need it." This covers you on a nightly basis.) I like unfussy food and rustic decor: taxidermy, vintage farmhouse tables. Admiring these things doesn't mean you have to admire rustic behavior. Like fashion, civility is contagious. And now we seem to be, unhappily, getting the dismal restaurant service we deserve.

You know how it will go, six times out of ten, once you've walked in a restaurant's door. There's no eye contact for the first five minutes. Once you're seated, you find that the table wobbles and the glassware is cloudy. When your meal arrives, waiters come by twice to ask if everything is all right before you've lifted your fork. My great friend Will likes to say that all one really wants from a server is that he or she be in a better mood than you are. I prize that observation. But it goes only so far.

Take, for example, the meal I had this fall at Fatty Crab, chef Zak Pelaccio's justifiably acclaimed pork- and seafood-minded, Malaysian-influenced restaurant in lower Manhattan. I love Pelaccio's food. His crispy pork and watermelon salad, a staple of his menu, still makes me happy I was put on earth. He has perfected a sensibility. He's a maestro. He practically makes you want to get a tattoo of a branzino on your forehead.

But it's mostly a soul-crushing experience to eat at Fatty Crab. It's cramped and dingy; the ten-ton thumping of the sous-chef's favorite Viking metal band pops your eardrums. Pelaccio's new cookbook is called *Eat with Your Hands*. At my meal I began to suspect he's urging us to do so because his cutlery and glassware are dirty. (New York City's department of health had given the restaurant one of its rare and off-putting "B" grades.)

Our waiter was kind and cheerful. But our table wobbled, and its surface was sticky. Drinks were pounded onto the table, cutlery flung toward us as if the waiter were playing craps. It's an attitude that infects, like an argument for nurture over nature, an entire room. Those who choose to eat at Fatty Crab must hunch over and yell to be heard. The yelling became braying. One oxford-shirted dandy held up a dripping Dungeness crab in his girlfriend's face. She pushed him, the way Elaine used to push Jerry. The crab flopped to the table, its claws cantilevered upward, as if begging for a chance to clip off the fellow's dainty earlobe. *Go, crab*, I thought. *Go*.

MANNERS MATTER, AND THERE'S SOMETHING ABOUT dismal service that sets bad manners in motion. These days eager waiters seem to be in competition with one another to commit that most fundamental of hapless bummers, that of clearing plates before everyone at the table has finished eating. More disastrously, hovering servers interrupt conversation to lift the bottle off the table to pour more wine into everyone's glass, right up to the top, even for those who don't want any more. The late Christopher Hitchens once took note of this moronic practice and asked, "How did such a barbaric custom get itself established, and why on earth do we put up with it?"

I like a meal at a restaurant bar counter, especially when I'm alone. But I'm wary about so many new restaurants insisting we eat at counters (no other type of seating is available), a movement that was jump-started by David Chang's Momofuku and its sister eateries. Chang's places get service right: brisk but warm and attentive. So does the counter-seating-only Manhattan restaurant Atera, where the food is mischievous and which deserves its two Michelin stars. But mostly the new counter-only places seem interested in hurting our backs and thus hurrying us along. I walked out of one of these restaurants after a meal with a friend not long ago. "You know," he said, "even Waffle Houses have tables." Many serious restaurants, of course, get service exactly right. But these tend to be the outliers—the 1 percent, not the 99—and the kind of place where a meal is a special occasion and will require an outlay of several hundred dollars. Take Per Se, for example, Thomas Keller's forward-thinking temple of gastronomy. "No first names, no flirting, no hands on the chairs, no touching the guest," Phoebe Damrosch wrote in her excellent memoir, *Service Included*, about working at Per Se. She added, "No cologne, scented lotions, scented soaps, aftershave or perfume." It's a funny book in praise of that most simple of human gifts: paying attention.

Or take Le Bernardin, which runs like a well-oiled minimalist clock. In his book *On the Line*, written with Christine Muhlke, Le Bernardin's chef and owner, Eric Ripert, listed 129 cardinal sins for servers. They should be studied by restaurant owners everywhere, even if they occasionally make Ripert sound overcaffeinated. Here's number 119: "No coffee in the saucer!!!!!!!!!!!!!!!!!!!!"

I recently had a meal at the revivified La Grenouille,* the venerable French restaurant on

* See "Host Nation," p. 26, written the following year.

East 52nd Street in Manhattan. What a beautiful room, what unfussy and understated service, in that cool French manner: there when you need it, invisible when you don't. You could sense the waiters' vibe infecting the room. When my wife needed a new fork, it appeared as if by magic. When a waiter committed what tennis players also call a service error—he dropped a plate quite loudly onto another one—no one in the restaurant even turned to gawk. This put me in mind of a friend, an older woman, who told me she was taught by her mother never to turn and look when there's a loud noise in a restaurant or anyplace else. "Why?" she asked. "Because it makes you look ugly," came the answer.

It's unfair to compare the service at Fatty Crab and La Grenouille. At the former, the waiters are would-be poets and musicians. At the latter, service is an esteemed career, and you can imagine Audrey Hepburn and Cary Grant at the next table. It's possible to eat there relatively inexpensively, too, especially in the pre-theater hours. Someone once objected to French manners, claiming they were all on the surface. James McNeill Whistler replied, "Well, you know, a very good place to have them."

It's important to visit a place like La Grenouille, so you can know what's missing.

I've gone on here a bit about restaurant service, as opposed to manners, because I'm trying to make the point that these things are interwoven. We don't expect even a modicum of the La Grenouille level of service anymore, and in large part, I think, it's because our own table manners have deteriorated. In his excellent 1946 study of advice books, *Learning How to Behave*, Arthur Schlesinger explained why civility and courtesy matter. "Even the outward motions," he wrote, "imply a certain kindliness and consideration for others." Schlesinger added that manners don't "complicate social life as much as they simplify it." He understood the best thing of all about good manners: They aren't snobby but egalitarian. They are open to all. They are free.

Over in England, where there is more left to preserve, they appear to be more worried about this deterioration than we are. British newspapers have noted that sales of table knives have plummeted because the fork-only eating of mushy food, in the American manner, has become dominant. One recent study of Britain's eating habits declared, as one horrified writer in the *Telegraph* reported, that

"Britons no longer worry about eating with their mouth closed, putting the knife and fork together when finished, or—most damning of all—keeping their elbows off the table."

In the best of all worlds, you learn your table manners at home, under the watchful eyes of your parents. If you've missed this variety of homeschooling, it's never too late to catch up. You can start today. The massive etiquette guidebooks from Emily Post and Amy Vanderbilt and Miss Manners have their place, but here's my advice. The book you should buy, today, from an independent bookseller, is one that deserves to be far better known. Its title is *Tiffany's Table Manners for Teenagers*, and it was written by Walter Hoving and first published in 1961.

It is short, unpretentious, beautifully illustrated, and exquisitely direct. It exists alongside Strunk and White's volume on literary style as a pocket-sized guidebook for life. It can be read in fifteen minutes, and then when you dine out others will gaze in your direction the way Grant did at Hepburn, and they will think, "Hasn't it occurred to you that I'm having a hard time keeping my hands off you?"

HOST NATION

BY HOLLY PETERSON

ARE HIGH-POWERED NEW YORKERS LOYAL
TO THEIR CANTEEN RINGMASTERS OR JUST
THE SOCIAL CIRCUS OF THEIR CITY?

O n a humid summer's eve this past June,
Charles Masson couldn't help tending to
the tightly packed peonies as he waited
for the well-turned-out crowd to celebrate him on
Manhattan's Upper East Side. Ten society women
were giving a party at Swifty's, a clubby little café
on Lexington Avenue, to honor his years running
La Grenouille, the restaurant from which he had
recently been banished by his family. Masson had
spent decades fussing over details and anticipating

every need of New York's most distinguished ladies and gentlemen, many living landmarks of a bygone era. This evening he must have felt a very strange kind of pre-dinner jumpiness as he fiddled around, early for his party, a guest in a restaurant that was not his own.

Shock waves had crashed against the cement shores of Park Avenue only weeks before, when it was announced that Masson's brother and mother had abruptly ousted him—for reasons unspecified—from his nearly four-decade perch as the face and host of La Grenouille, a dining establishment that was born in the French haute cuisine heyday of Le Pavillon, La Côte Basque, La Caravelle, and Lutèce—all since shuttered. "We thought it would be nice, when he felt a bit lost and shell-shocked, to throw him a party," said Elizabeth Peabody, one of the hostesses. "It was about seventy people, almost everyone you know in New York."

La Grenouille, many say, continued to exist only because of Masson and his highly mannered yet unobtrusive way with patrons. He always welcomed guests like cherished relatives before they even sat for their seared foie gras with quince or quenelles of pike Lyonnaise with caviar. Susan Burke, who spearheaded the event honoring Masson, summed up the sentiment of his following: "Manhattan's a really small town in some ways. None of my friends are going to La Grenouille anymore. They'll be fine. They'll have out-of-towners. It will just be a very different place."

New York's restaurant landscape is dotted with exclusive establishments where it's unclear whether the allure is the scene inside or the manager who created it. It's no surprise that the ten women hosting the party for Masson chose Swifty's. Pretenders who get reservations there won't feel like (God forbid) out-of-towners, but they might not feel they quite fit in, either. "New Yorkers like clubs because they like to be a member of something," Swifty's co-owner Robert Caravaggi says. He worked with the inimitable Glenn Bernbaum, who ran Mortimer's, the legendary Upper East Side *boîte*, like a private club. When Bernbaum died, Mortimer's closed. The crowd nested safely at Swifty's. "We are not an official club," Caravaggi says, "but we enjoy being around like-minded people. It has a lot to do with tradition and friendship. These people have an affection for me and my co-owner, Stephen Attoe, and we try to return it to them."

Society columnist Liz Smith, who has frequented every New York hot spot from El Morocco on, explains: "Restaurant-going at Manhattan's top level has always been about playing to people's illusions that they are able to eat in expensive places and know who everyone is around them." The symbiotic relationship between patron and gregarious owner only intensifies the creation of an inner circle—elite members who get special treatment—above the hoi polloi. Without that relationship, a restaurant, even a great one, is just a place to eat.

"People follow people," says Tina Brown, CEO of Tina Brown Live Media and one of the city's most successful conveners. "It's all about the maître d'. It's not about the place. It's that personal touch of the *bon vivant* who greets you, who knows you want to sit on the corner bench on the left, who understands you hate it when you're given too many choices and will give you your baked potato with olive oil even before you ask for it, and knows you love lime juice and soda to keep you cool when it's hot."

Though New York likes to project the Emma Lazarus image that it is open to all, many of its restaurants have stringent rules that endlessly confound us. "There are de facto clubs, and it's unclear what the rules are," says Michael Wolff, author and media analyst. "You don't know how to get into nightclubs, much less into these restaurants that have become this sort of portal. It's weird: Restaurants are public places, in business to feed people, and, at the same time, people fear they can't get in." The host provides the entrée.

On the Manhattan restaurant scene, this much is clear: The more family- (and lineage-) oriented Upper East Side restaurants tend to cater to a set crowd, while the power lunch establishments recognize more of a meritocracy ladder of haute accomplishers. In the spectacular coliseum that is the Philip Johnson–designed Four Seasons Grill Room, the men and women who pretty much run New York like to sit at quiet tables about two feet from the other gladiators. Seen and not heard is the object as they conspire to merge some institutions and take down others.

"Something is always going on at the Four Seasons Grill Room," Smith says. "I don't think anyone knows who the chef is. The guys running it"—hosts Julian Niccolini and Alex von Bidder—"have become famous for their outrageous behavior." Niccolini and von

Bidder spend every weekday morning placing the powerful at appropriate tables, in a complex game of musical chairs. "They are funny and sexy and make people feel at home," she says. "Patrons come because it's easy to get to, and it's a great place to talk business. If Julian left it would be terrible—and it's hard to tell what would survive."*

Society people gravitate more to the manager who understands where the overlap is between an Upper East Side den and a country club. The powerful like a convivial and famous greeter like Julian or Alex, who understands the delicate seesaw of jocular insubordination and obsequiousness—but let's face it, the people in this group are also drawn to one another. With dozens of world-class restaurants in Manhattan, many of the Four Seasons regulars return several times a week to the same booth and even the same thirty-five-dollar baked potato made to their liking, as if the Four Seasons were their personal commissary.

The power lunch spots further diverge between business and media. Journalist (and executive producer of *Veep*) Frank Rich remembers a time early

---

* Following a series of public clashes with landlord Aby Rosen, the Four Seasons left the Seagram Building at the end of July 2016, when the restaurant's lease expired.

in his career, at *Time* magazine in the 1970s, when "lunch was a huge part of the culture. Top editors like Henry Grunwald would go to La Caravelle all the time. My back-of-the-book editor and I would have lunch almost every day. She knew the owner of Chez Napoléon—it's still there, in the West 50s— and we'd have long lunches and we'd discuss what we were writing and everything that was going on in the magazine." Though Rich notes that technology has made doing editorial business over lunch less common, the tradition still prevails in publishing, magazines, and television. There is what is essentially a big cafeteria where you can find all the *machers*: Michael's, on West 55th Street. It's hard to determine if it's owner Michael McCarty himself or his general manager, Steve Millington, who commands the crowd, or if everyone in the media is just drawn to this locale, like bugs to a porch light. "It's a function of recognition," McCarty says. "It's more of a human relationship than a financial one. Each day we go in there, we put together a fantastic seating, and then it's showtime, it's theater."

"From a functional point of view it's efficient," says Wolff, who had a public feud with Michael's

managers, boycotted the place for a few years, and is
now back enjoying his front-and-center table. "You
know the people who are going to be there, the people
who are interesting and helpful to see. If you do that,
and then you go into a restaurant where you don't
know anyone, you kind of feel gypped. What do I get
out of this? Just a bowl of pasta?" Imagine that: going
to a restaurant for the purpose of having a wonderful
bowl of pasta.

In New York in particular, visibility is survival.
People don't drive on Manhattan's cluttered
avenues, so they can't show off their expensive cars.
Apartments, while sometimes palatial, are entombed
in concrete fourteen floors up behind a doorman's
watch and not landscaped for a Beverly Hills tourist
bus to gawk at. If people keep seeing you out and
about, if they spot you at your corner table enjoying
your frisée salad the way you like it—light on the
lardons—they discern that you are actually okay.
New York is such a manic, frenetic city that there's
comfort in familiar faces. Those who have penetrated
the magic circle want to remain inside it while the
going is good. And if the going isn't so good, being
inside that cocoon makes them feel as if it might be

again soon. Hosts like Masson, Niccolini, von Bidder, McCarty, and Caravaggi are there to assure them, either way.

The ousted Charles Masson, for his part, has plans to open a French restaurant this December at the Baccarat Hotel and will no doubt work hard at his special brand of tending-to. He is aware that people have been resisting the call of those La Grenouille quenelles with caviar because he is not there to greet them, but he addresses the matter in elegant character. "There's no reason to boycott La Grenouille, because that would be punishing the very employees that I worked with," he says. "We built something beautiful, and there's no point in dismantling it." He will try to recapture it, and his faithful crowd. Will they follow? No one who was at the party at Swifty's that night would ever underestimate the loyalty of a hungry Upper East Side army.*

* Masson left Chevalier at the Baccarat Hotel in 2015. He is reportedly involved with a new restaurant at the Lowell Hotel, set to open in 2016.

THE
ME DIET

BY JOE KEENAN

WHEN DID "YOU ARE WHAT YOU EAT" BECOME
"YOU ARE WHAT YOU'RE TOLD TO EAT"?
ONE SELF-HELP HOLDOUT QUESTIONS THE
WISDOM OF THE PERSONAL NUTRITIONIST.

We live in an age when those seeking physical and spiritual perfection do not lack for paid guidance. Hordes of experts and gurus stand ready to help us enhance any aspect of our beings that we find wanting and to ensure that, whether we succeed or fall short, our efforts will not be lonely. Given the intimate nature of their services, it is no surprise that many people come to view their most valued instructors as friends, confidants, or even soul mates. This affection is often warmly returned, especially when the client is well connected in publishing circles or, better still, Oprah.

Though these best-loved helpers have been with us for ages, the duties they perform have varied with changing times and fashions. Back in the 1930s, socialites were smitten with their psychiatrists, a new sort of doctor whose brilliance was signaled by his inability to find anything you told him uninteresting. In more recent years we've lost our hearts to fitness trainers, yoga teachers, and life coaches. But the red-hot darling of the moment is, without question, the personal nutritionist.

I have never consulted a personal nutritionist myself, though I have certainly wondered if I might benefit from seeing one. The question looms largest each January, which is also when I loom largest, but so far I have resisted making an appointment, partly because I'm a late adopter who seldom boards a bandwagon till the parade's nearly done and the banners are drooping sadly, but mostly because I've had no idea what a personal nutritionist actually does.

I have since researched the matter and learned a good deal, but I believe my initial confusion was pardonable. Isn't all the information we need to make smart food choices freely available from numerous sources? Ten years ago the thought of hiring your own expert would have struck most of us as a pointless extravagance, like having a personal weatherman to tell you when it was raining out. Why, then, are personal nutritionists so popular now? How did they rise so swiftly? And what does our embrace of them say about us? The answers dwell somewhere in that murky zone where Health and High Purpose collide with Vanity and Status, our loftiest impulses blending with our lowest until they're as hard to separate as the berries in a smoothie.

Americans' relationship to food was not always the fraught, mistrustful affair it is today. Once, we ate what we liked and gave little thought to nutrition science, seeing the word *nutritious* as synonymous with *edible*. This changed in the mid-seventies, when doctors with diet books to sell started claiming that certain kinds of calories made us fatter than others. If the doctors disagreed about which calories were at fault, at least we all learned what carbs were. Then the Internet arrived and started bombarding us daily with new hotly contested theories. Now the debates weren't just about which foods would make you fat; they were about which foods would make you fat, then *kill* you.

Was sugar toxic? Was eating gluten just slow suicide by bagel? And if so, which regimen would save you? The Paleo Diet, which permits only those foods consumed by the first hunter-gatherers? Or the Raw Food Diet, in which nothing can be cooked? Was our first wrong turn at agriculture—or earlier still, at fire?

Amid such uncertainty it's easy to see why people warmed to the idea of having their own food arbiter, someone whose judgment was rendered sound by the fee it commanded. And one can't overlook the appeal of the job title itself. Those seeking to distinguish themselves from lesser beings have long been drawn to adjectives like *personal* and *private*. Think of the luster they add to such words as *chef*, *shopper*, and *concierge*, to say nothing of *elevator*, *plane*, and *beach*. Imagine the thrill the early adopters must have felt as they extolled their new hires to uninitiated friends: *The salsa looks great, but I can't touch the corn chips. Wendy says corn is the devil. Wendy? Oh, she's my personal nutritionist. Well, not just mine. Sting uses her, too.*

If novelty helped nutritionists win their first converts, they owe their lasting popularity to their reputations as all-purpose healers. Since (as they assure us) most human ailments stem from a flawed diet, it follows that an improved, properly supervised diet will banish our ills, restoring us to that cheerfully energetic state that is all mankind's birthright but is now seldom glimpsed outside of musicals.

Some nutritionists go further, claiming that their diets confer spiritual benefits as well. Dr. Alejandro Junger, the author of *Clean Gut*, markets a twenty-one-day detox kit that gives his followers the same pious joy that ascetics and holy men of old felt as they starved their way into God's good graces. The booming market for these cleanses and flushes, combined with the renewed popularity of enemas, has led some skeptics to point out that the digestive tract, with its trillions of flora and bacteria, can hardly be made to gleam and sparkle like a Tesla showroom, but such arguments can't dampen the fervor of those who insist on conflating the state of their souls with that of their colons.

A good nutritionist also makes you feel you're a force for positive societal change. We live in an alarmingly fat nation, a place where greedy Big Food companies reap billions by pumping calories that are mostly empty into people who are seldom full. Having a nutritionist shows that you're not among the benighted hordes driving up health care costs by avoiding kale while viewing mayonnaise as a beverage. You're part of the solution, not the problem, which you can demonstrate by entertaining your dinner guests with fun facts about alkaline balances or the enteric nervous system, the "second brain" that we all have in our stomach linings but that few of us know about, let alone really listen to. If your efforts to explain this after a cocktail lead friends to wonder if you've overstated the number of brains you contain by two, then no matter. One glance at your slim physique will confirm that your nutritionist clearly knows his enzymes.

And you *will* be thin. Not that it matters. No, really. Yes, some clients may need help in paring down a truly unfortunate circumference, but dieting is so . . . *yesterday*, so shallow. Today it's all about *wellness* and *energy*, though some weight loss may result once you renounce sugar, wheat, and other poisons and start to view parsley less as a garnish and more as an entrée. *I swear I had no idea how much weight I'd lost until I put on my old Chanel suit and it literally fell off me. You always admired that suit. Would you like it?*

But the biggest reason people love personal nutritionists is that they're so, well, personal. Their advice, unlike any to be found in a book, is individually tailored to you and your fabulously quirky stomach. Your nutritionist invites you to see your digestive workings as a gripping detective story, one in which each cramp, energy dip, and mood swing is a crime with a culprit to be tracked down and apprehended. His zeal is commendable, though it does lead certain clients to assume that the details of this gastric inquest are compelling not just to themselves but to anyone who likes a good mystery. *I felt so lethargic every Sunday afternoon and couldn't think why. And you know what it was? The cream cheese I was eating at brunch! Not the cheese itself, mind you—the scallions!*

Whenever I hear these food laments, I can't help noticing how much delight the victims seem to derive from each new Achilles' heel they discover. To be clear, I'm not talking about the sort of dire food allergies that can lead to EpiPens, emergency room trips, and, on occasion, eulogies. I mean those milder conditions that occupy the middle range between "yuck" and death. Though they're hard to verify medically, people seem to speak of these weaknesses with a beleaguered pride that always reminds me of the fairy tale "The Princess and the Pea." In the musical version, *Once Upon a Mattress*, the queen describes her own rarefied nature in song:

Sensitivity, sensitivity,
I'm just loaded with that.
In this one word is the epitome
Of the aristocrat.
Sensitive soul and sensitive stomach,
Sensitive hands and feet;
This is the blessing, also the curse of
Being the true elite.

THESE DAYS THE PRINCESS WOULD BE EXPECTED TO both feel the pea under twenty mattresses and discern that it was genetically modified.

Nutritionists understand our need to be heroes in our own stories, to wage battle against the forces that stand between us and our best selves. They know, too, that when it comes to bragging rights, intestinal fortitude is no match for intestinal delicacy. If we could consume just anything with no ill effect, what would we be? Lobsters? Human garbage pails? *Anthony Bourdain?*

Fashions are fickle, and no helper can stay the hot new thing forever. Nutritionists, like trainers before them, are growing popular across all social strata, winning fresh converts while diluting their prestige among the trendsetters who started it all. Undaunted, these lifestyle pioneers are already scanning the horizon for the next must-have human accessory. If you're among those searching, you can stop looking right now. It's farmers.

Seriously. For years now growers have been cozying up to posh restaurants and celebrity chefs. (Those who scoff at the idea of humble farmers harboring social ambitions should remember that they're the ones who started calling tomatoes "heirlooms.") Now private citizens are striking their own deals, snapping up all the artisanal veggies and scarce salad greens they can. Some of this produce is sold at prices that make one ask if the fennel is watered with Evian and the eggs are by Fabergé, but for the buyers it's all well worth it when they sit down with their guests for that first glorious high summer brunch. *Try the corn—it's amazing! . . . Hm? Well, that's just nonsense. Corn is not bad for you! Not when it comes from Zeke. Zeke? Oh, he's my personal farmer.*

Chapter 2

MONEY

WHAT MAKES THE RICH BEG?

BY CHRISTINE LENNON

WHEN IT COMES TO THE ADMISSIONS PROCESS
FOR PRIVATE SCHOOLS, IT'S BEST TO REMEMBER
TWO RULES: SILENCE IS GOLDEN, AND YOUR
CHECKBOOK BETTER BE, TOO.

We've all heard the stories. The friend of a friend who wrote a $50,000 check from the maternity ward to secure Junior's spot in the high school graduating class of 2030. The couple that built a library/parking structure/music room as a well-meaning gesture after they toured the school and "saw a need." Then there's the one about the admissions director who pointed to two stacks of paperwork on her desk and said, "This is the pile of candidates we're considering. Yours is in the other one."

Over the past eighteen months these tales have tagged along with me as I toured twelve private schools, attended open houses, and simulated playdates with my five-year-old twins, who on one occasion cavorted in a schoolyard with numbers pinned to their shirts like livestock at a state fair, all in the name of kindergarten admission.

We live in Los Angeles, a city where the private school process is just as cutthroat as in New York, as it is in Chicago, San Francisco, and Atlanta. The incessant babble about where little Wolfie or Juniper or Harlow (remember, I live in L.A.) will learn to hold a pencil correctly, to the tune of $25,000 per year, often includes the terms *fund-raising*, *development*, *advancement*, and *capital campaigns*. In a word: money.

Money is not my native language, which explains why I'm a writer, not a hedge fund manager. So I needed a crash course in private school economics. What are the real financial expectations of the families applying to private schools these days? If trying to buy your way into a prestigious school is so frowned upon, how do the shameless 1-percenters whose bank accounts are their best shot at gaining entry let their philanthropic enthusiasm be known? And then, once those of us who don't have the means to build a new wing are (hopefully) accepted by a school, what are the expectations for giving beyond tuition?

The first rule of private school fund-raising is to not acknowledge that it exists; just let the elephant linger unacknowledged, throughout the admissions process. If a school mentions plans for a new gym, an improved art studio, or a cutting-edge science lab, the appropriate response is to marvel at the sleek plans and project how your budding young chemist Orson would thrive in such a facility. Scoffing at the cost, or volunteering to front it, is not advised. "I know for a fact that the top-tier schools in Los Angeles will not accept donations from a family that is participating in the admissions process," says Michelle Nitka, a clinical psychologist and author of *Coping with Preschool Panic*, who counsels clients on private school entry.

But the reality is that at least 5 percent of each class, whether it's at a K–6 elementary school, a two-century-old boarding school, or a small liberal arts college, is "targeted for development" by administrators, meaning that it's picked for admission in part because of an assumed generosity. ("If a school is in the middle of a big capital campaign, then it's possible for that number to be higher," says Nitka.)

Someone has to buy all those Bunsen burners, or fill the financial aid coffers—it's just the talking-about-it part that feels icky, so if you're determined to communicate that you have a fat wallet and are itching to share, let someone else do it for you. "We advise clients to have someone, ideally an ethical person who is close to the school, contact a trustee or someone in admissions or development and say, 'I have a friend or colleague who's applying to a school with their child, and did you know that they are the daughter of so-and-so, because their name might not ring a bell?'" says Suzanne Rheault, founder of Aristotle Circle, a New York–based business that connects families with admissions advisers and tutors for students applying at any level, from elementary school to graduate school. "Or, 'I just want to alert you to the fact that this family, in the past, has been extremely generous with their community.'"

There are infinite ways for schools to learn about their applicants and to ferret out who the potential big givers are without saying a word, thanks to the vast amount of information available online. Did you write your address on the application? Then you have Zillow.com to thank for revealing how much you paid for your home and when. Did you post pictures from your two-week Amangani vacation on Facebook? Kill at the box office? It's all just a Google away.

But what if you ask someone for an endorsement and then decide not to enroll your child? Rheault and Nitka caution clients against asking someone to go to bat for you unless it's your first or second choice, so as not to burn a critical bridge for, say, another of your children. And if you do change your mind, contact the person who referred you immediately to break the news.

"Honesty is important. If you can, you say, 'This school is amazing, and in the end it's going to come down to this school and that school.' At least they know there's a possibility you won't accept," Rheault says. "If it's your fifth choice, don't put that person in that position."

Nitka recommends notifying the person who referred you to graciously explain in detail why you chose another school (it's single-gender, has better athletics, has a stronger math program, etc.) and sending a brief but thoughtful note to the school you rejected—or more. "To help assuage any bad feelings, make a donation to the school that you were accepted to but decided not to attend. It doesn't have to be a lot," she says. "It's a good faith gesture. It helps save a friendship and some credibility."

Once the acceptance letters start to roll in, including one from your school of choice, hopefully, so do the calls for donations. It may be difficult to accept the fact that the steep tuition simply does not cover the costs of running the school, but it's true. Every school needs generous families. Several anonymous sources said that an additional 10 percent of the tuition is a good guideline for a family of more moderate means to follow when it comes to fund-raising. Typically a school will appoint a few willing families in the community to solicit money from the others, or hire a development officer to do the dirty work, and they usually suggest an actual dollar amount. One friend, an established screenwriter who is a parent at our twins' new school, says he got a call from a colleague of his agent's suggesting a donation in the solid seven-figure zone. "I said, 'If you work with my agent, you should know I can't afford that,'" he says with a laugh.

My husband and I got our first call of this nature almost exactly one month into the new school year. The twins were accepted to our top choice and a couple of others, by some minor miracle. We hadn't offered a penny to any of them before, and if our history of giving to the nerdiest environmental nonprofits was what secured two spots on the coveted roster, I'd be surprised. I'd like to think that our cherubic children wrangled their own entry with their significant charms. Just last week I got a little misty-eyed as I imagined how they'll shine over the years, blossoming into well-adjusted adolescents in such an idyllic school environment, as I tasted the tang of envelope glue on my tongue and dropped the fund-raising check into the mail slot.

A
FAREWELL
TO ALMS

BY KEVIN CONLEY

ARE ALL THE NEWFANGLED, GLAMOROUS
WAYS OF DOING PHILANTHROPY PUTTING
AN END TO PLAIN OLD GIVING?

*V*enture philanthropy is trending in do-
gooder circles. The hybrid term has its
roots in the venture capital movement,
an investment technique pioneered in Silicon
Valley, where tech-savvy zillionaires have been
plowing their own stashes back into start-ups for
four decades. But after hundreds of TED talks
and NYC rooftop bar open-mike elevator pitch
sessions, venture capitalism has now evolved into
a quantifiable business strategy, spawning huge
investment companies such as Kleiner Perkins and

Peter Thiel's Founders Fund, a kind of West Coast alternative to hedge funds.

Along the way, venture capitalists formalized the approach, demanding things like regular progress reports, Skype sessions with founders, and quarterly updates in exchange for their checks. Eventually they started applying identical riders when they gave money to nonprofits, taking proven business efficiencies they learned while moving start-ups to IPOs and transferring them to water projects in Rwanda and famine relief in Ethiopia.

But if the elaborate, MBA-style principles of venture philanthropy, with its focus on measurable results, are currently in, then charity, that old-fashioned urge to give money directly to the poor and those in need—the sort of problem that resists solution by spreadsheet (or financial jiggery-pokery)—is definitely out, mocked by the VC and angel-investor cohort as feel-good social-ego philanthropy indulged in for immediate praise.

Maybe it's time to rethink that. Numerous studies suggest that great wealth has a tendency to isolate the individuals it enriches. The rich may give more overall, but they give about 50 percent less as a proportion of their income than their middle- and working-class counterparts. Precise figures vary from survey to survey, but on average the poorest 20 percent give from 3.6 percent to 4.7 percent of their income and the top 20 percent from 1.7 to 2.8 percent. Some of this is simply a matter of opportunity: The less well-off are a lot more likely to come into contact with those in need, so they have more chances to exercise compassion. But there's also evidence that those who live in splendid isolation are simply not the giving type. In one study after another, those with greater advantages take more candy, don't stop for pedestrians, give fewer dollars, and reach for their phones during testimonials from those with cancer.

A few trendsetters, starting with the latest pope, are pushing charity back into the headlines. During his Easter week debut, Francis, the first New World pope, who has given up the red loafers of his predecessor in favor of plain black shoes, shocked many in the old guard by washing the feet of twelve juvenile prisoners, two of them women, during a Holy Thursday service. This ancient gesture of humility—Christ did the same thing for the apostles at the Last Supper—reaffirmed the message he was sending by taking the name Francis, patron saint of the poor. When, in his first official published interview, Pope Francis suggested that the church had been excessively focused on gays and abortion at the expense of serving the poor and marginalized, even the most casual Vatican watcher started to wonder, *Is the Pope Catholic?*

There is evidence that charity is now challenging the recent ascendancy of venture philanthropy and even gaining backers in Silicon Valley. In 2012 the nonprofit start-up Watsi attracted funding from the VC investment firm Y Combinator; it was the first time the firm, which was one of the original backers of Dropbox and Reddit and usually trades seed money for 6 percent of future profits, had ever backed a nonprofit. Watsi uses the same crowd-funding strategy as Kickstarter, the New York City–based website that allows people to seek online donations by posting pitches for projects in film, music, theater, or business. And this online catalog of appeals helps Watsi get needed money directly to the sick and poor all over the globe. Pictures of real people and their stories (Stephanie, from Kenya, is a twelve-year-old who wants to grow up to be a writer but needs reconstructive surgery) are posted beside Kickstarter-style numbers (20 percent funded, $1,195 to go). "Technology can now put a face on need," Y Combinator co-founder Paul Graham said.

Can charity go viral? One recent runaway success suggests just that. After Aaron Collins, a healthy but troubled thirty-year-old, committed suicide, his family followed a request in his will urging them to go out to dinner somewhere and "leave an awesome tip (and I don't mean 25 percent. I mean $500 on a fucking pizza) for a waiter or waitress." A video of the giving of that $500 tip, to a waitress at Puccini's Smiling Teeth in Lexington, Kentucky, was quickly reposted on Gawker, Videogum, Yahoo, Reddit, and many more sites (the startled twentysomething fans herself and says, "Are you kidding me?" over and over) and raised more than $50,000 in a month for still more awesome tips.

All the great faiths champion regular giving to the poor as a sacred obligation, one that benefits both of the souls involved in the transaction. Medical studies suggest that the benefits are not just spiritual: Those who give experience a helper's high, with hormonal benefits similar to those from exercise. Perhaps this explains why individuals who give to charity on their own out-donate corporations and family foundations by a margin of three to one.

What does charity look like in action? At a recent dinner for Rolls-Royce, I ran into a father and his eighth-grade son, each of whom had his favorite style of Rolls, and they were teasing each other about their preferences. Given their easy banter, I wasn't surprised to find that the father, Robert Jafari, who had made a variety of fortunes in medical supplies and construction (and lost a fortune or two in casinos along the way), had set up a series of programs designed to quietly give money to families in need.

He had written his own mission statement, but it turned out that much of his giving was based simply on listening to the people who worked in his companies—who, Jafari said, were a lot more likely to know people in trouble than he was. When he began chatting with a maid who cleaned his offices, for instance, he found out that she was in fact a nun, Sister Maria Trinity, from Veracruz, Mexico, and she had come north to earn money, which she sent back to a home for the abandoned elderly and the terminally ill that her order ran in Xalapa. "With the money I earn here," she told him, "it's like hiring five people down there." That encounter began charitable donations that have continued for nearly twenty years.

"They don't want to ask for money," he said. "I have to remind them to call me before they run out. They'll say, 'We waited until we had enough peanut butter for the patients but not for the sisters.' I have to tell them, 'Call me sooner. I can't give if I don't know.'"

MAID
OF
MILLIONS

BY ALEXANDRA WOLFE

WHAT DOES IT MEAN WHEN THE WEALTHY
LEAVE THEIR MONEY NOT TO FAMILY BUT TO A
BELOVED PET OR HOUSEKEEPER? THE ANSWER'S
MORE COMPLICATED THAN IT APPEARS.

O
n May 24, 2011, in a secured wing of Beth
Israel Hospital in Manhattan, a woman
known as Harriet Chase died at the age
of 104. And when the will of Harriet Chase (who
was really the heiress Huguette Clark) was filed
the following month, it revealed that she had left
much of her half-billion-dollar estate to charity and
potentially tens of millions to her longtime caretaker,
Hadassah Peri. It was a bequest that raised a question
that had been asked of millionaires before her: Why

leave money to the maid if you haven't pulled an *Ahh*-nold?

Clark joins a line of lonely figures who have replaced family with the proverbial Jeeves or Fido. Mark Rothko, Doris Duke, and Leona Helmsley were, like Clark, wealthy people who made one of their grandest statements posthumously. Rothko left most of his works to his foundation, not his children. Duke left much of her billion-dollar estate to her eponymous foundation. And Helmsley, of course, left $12 million to her Maltese, Trouble, who died in June of 2011.

Although Helmsley was widely ridiculed, four-legged beneficiaries are hardly uncommon. Singer Dusty Springfield arranged for her cat Nicholas to sleep on a mattress covered by her nightgown. Countess Karlotta Liebenstein left her German shepherd, Gunther III, $65 million. (The money then passed to his son, Gunther IV.) Actress Beryl Reid left her five cats her $1.8 million house. Such gifts, says famed lawyer Ed Hayes, usually mean one thing: "They're estranged from their children."

Oddly, leaving your money to your dog can actually be easier than leaving it to your staff. After all, no one can accuse your poodle of manipulation. In fact, any outside parties named in wills face a fair amount of scrutiny. When socialite Gail Posner died in 2010 and left $27 million to her staff, including $5 million to her puppy sitter, her son protested. He may have heard stories like the one about Marlon Brando, whose former maid sued for $100 million, claiming that she and the actor had been lovers and had agreed to split his money when his time came.

But *Richistan* author Robert Frank sees another meaning behind this growing tide of people who don't leave their money to their offspring. It's not that they're estranged from their children—it's that they want to encourage them to make their own way. Warren Buffett, Bill Gates, and Sandy Weill have all said that inheriting wealth takes away children's drive. "Money can become a vehicle for emotional punishment and reward within families," Frank says. "Today's wealthy are very aware of how wealth can damage their kids."

That may be so, but try telling that to Clark's two half-grandnieces and one half-grandnephew, to whom she didn't leave a cent. How good a case do they have if they try to contest the will?* Not great, says lawyer Francis Harvey, Jr., who co-represented Andy Warhol's estate.

* According to the details of the 2013 settlement, the estranged family was awarded $34.5 million, while Ms. Peri had to pay back $5 million to Clark's estate.

"People rarely challenge a will's [content]," he says. Often, spurned family members' only recourse is to challenge the mental state of the deceased loved one at the time of signature. And that too will be difficult for Clark's heirs to establish. Although Clark's attorney, Wallace Bock, tried many times to get her to sign a will naming him as a beneficiary, he was blocked by her family after the media picked up on the $1.5 million gift Clark had given him to build a bomb shelter for his daughter, who lived in an Israeli settlement. Bock, along with Clark's accountant, sex offender Irving Kamsler, ended up with only $500,000 apiece and roles as co-directors of her foundation.

But in the end Clark may simply have been more particular than she appeared. For instance, she did single out one family intimate as a beneficiary: a goddaughter, to whom she left several million. And while popular opinion has painted her a victim of her lawyer—or her own decrepitude—she may have protected herself better than most people assumed. Clark lived in America for more than eighty years, but she was born in Paris and spoke mostly in French so interlopers couldn't understand her. Not a bad idea. In a world where dogs are richer than people, family squabbles might soon be solved in Swahili.

RICH YOU, POOR ME

BY HENRY ALFORD

WHEN FRIENDSHIPS SPAN SOCIOECONOMIC
DIVIDES, THE POSSIBLE PITFALLS ARE MANY.
AND THEY MUST BE NAVIGATED WITH CARE.

S ome years ago, two friends and I decided to
meet for dinner at a favorite French bistro,
where we hoped to find the joy located at the
intersection of lardons and malbec. My boyfriend
was out of town at the time, so I thought I might
ask my friend Jane, because I knew the four of us
would hit it off. But then I remembered that Jane
is a freelance book reviewer and that my two other
friends' penchant for $125 bottles of wine might lie
outside Jane's budget. It was too late to suggest a more
affordable restaurant. So, what to do?

Part of me thought, *I simply won't ask Jane—I don't want to set in motion a chain of events that might lead her to conclude that she is lesser than anyone.* But another part of me thought, *Isn't this Jane's decision to make for herself?* So I sent her an e-mail explaining the situation. Jane politely declined, claiming a full dance card. As the days passed, I grew more and more convinced that she'd declined for financial reasons. Simultaneously I realized that part of why I wanted Jane on board was that she'd be the perfect foil to my friend Edward's wine-fueled verbal onslaughts. I wondered if politesse would permit me to pay for Jane's meal? I decided yes—as long as I presented the offer as a birthday present. Which I did. But she demurred again. Finally I called Jane and put more cards—not just the birthday card—on the table. I explained that I wanted her to be my bulwark against the flames of the fiery Edward-dragon. She finally rallied, shiny sword in hand. A birthday was celebrated; malbec was swilled. The four of us had a fabulous evening.

There's a small tap dance that we perform when we make plans with people who are either much wealthier or much less wealthy than we. We hope this dance will be nimble and Astaire-like, but more often it comes across as darty-eyed and sweaty.

Granted, we more commonly encounter the rich/ poor axis in relation to family or employees: Your assistant is going to Paris, so you give her an Hermès scarf so she can wow her Parisian hosts on arrival; your nephew is in town for two nights, so you offer to take him and his new girlfriend out for the first non-pizza meal of their union. In either of these situations, the rich/poor problem isn't really a problem; *noblesse oblige* compels you to cough up, so you do. Any slight awkwardness is purely a matter of your assistant's insistence on wearing the scarf on her head in a way that screams *Rhoda*.

But when the axis pops up in situations involving friends, the going gets tougher. Occasionally people employ practical steps that help to blur the financial dissonance and to put everyone at ease. I loved it when a friend I'd asked to recommend a real estate agent gave me two names—one who mostly handles houses "approaching and surpassing $1 million" and one whose listings were more modest. I loved it when, on an occasion when a group of friends was holing up at a rented house for a stretch of time, one person magically stocked the house with food and subsequently started pimping some of his own culinary creations. I love it when people who learn I'm going on a trip—particularly if they're chic or frequent-flying—ask me, "What neighborhood are you staying in?" rather than "Where are you staying?" The latter question seems to beg the response "The Ritz. I know of no other location."

But are there any larger principles here that might help us tackle the vagaries? Two suggest themselves. First, offers of birthday celebrations notwithstanding, it's best if we don't make an exception of the impecunious person. If your weekend in the country includes a glamorous balloon trip that will set each person back $500, then it's lovely if you yourself (or some other member of the party) hang back with Mr. Cash-Strapped so that, come sunset, he isn't the only tiny ant on the landscape. Second, we can reduce most financial awkwardness if we take an ironic or comic approach to the fanciness of the occasion in question. "Of course, we all need to go horseback riding and wear the inn's collection of top hats: We're practicing for our Currier and Ives portrait." "I think it's absolutely imperative that we each rent our own beach cabana—you never know what you might pick up from someone else's shade."

And what are we to do when the tables are turned, and we are the relatively poor? Here it's probably valid and useful to speak candidly and tell people you're on a budget, or that vintage Lamborghini rentals are beyond your reach. But the trick is to do so without sounding like Al Gore at a plastics convention. Self-deprecation is a welcome addition here: "That sounds so lovely, but I think I better say no. I've been feeling a little Dorothea Lange recently, and I'm really trying to hone my grimness." Or go even grittier: "I think I better bow out—I'm counting pennies due To a recent spate of Al-Pacino-in-*Scarface*-in-front-of-a-hillock-of-cocaine-type behavior." A path will open for you.

It's also possible to work toward compromise by asking your host or friend the right questions. "Would it be weird if I just met you after the concert for a drink?" "Is there anyone else going to Nantucket that weekend who might want to share a hotel room?" "What if, instead of going on the weekend, I drove everyone and their luggage to JFK and en route we all had a send-off meal at that terrific Thai place in Queens?"

It can help, too, to remember that most of us have friends or a friend whose fabulousness renders us seemingly poor by comparison, even though we're in the same socioeconomic group: the colleague with the gorgeous sailboat who just married a twenty-five-years-younger-than-you Croatian model; the friend who works for Clear Channel who is always slipping you the front-row Lady Gaga tickets he can't use. Whenever we consort with these folks, it's an opportunity for us to either start circling the drain of insecurity or greed, or figure out what commodities we have with which to return the favor. Do your friends covet the silk-screen T-shirts you make—the ones with all the sea anemones and the tentacles and the labial frill? Or maybe they love your gameness and constant availability, the way you're still answering your phone at eleven p.m.? Or it's your crazy potty-mouthed Eighty-eight-year-old mother and her retinue of hilariously inappropriate men, isn't it? That's why people love you.

Whatever it is, you probably have some commodity that has value in the economy of your friendship. This commodity is something to trade on. Because, in the end, the differences between you and your Hamptons manse–renting friend can be eased and abated by a variant of Marxism. From each according to his ability; to each according to his envy.

THE SOREST LOSER

BY ALEXANDRA STYRON

THE SAGA OF THE WINKLEVOSS TWINS
ILLUSTRATES A NEW AMERICAN AXIOM:
IF AT FIRST YOU DON'T SUCCEED,
WHINE, WHINE AGAIN.

*"One of the first businesses of a sensible man
is to know when he is beaten, and
to leave off fighting at once."*
—SAMUEL BUTLER

In the annals of the aggrieved, nobody has it over
Hans Kohlhase. A figure of German legend,
Kohlhase was a sixteenth-century Brandenburg
merchant who was taking his wares to the Leipzig
fair one day when he found himself detained by the
servants of a Saxon nobleman. The men, as was their

brutish custom, demanded Kohlhase's horses. Kohlhase complied, though the inconvenience cost him precious time and money. When, as he was heading home, the lackeys tried to exact a toll for the horses' return, the merchant balked. Finally, seeing no other way out, he paid the fee, but vowed to seek redress in a court of law. The courts failed him. Furious, Kohlhase set out on a course of revenge against not only the nobleman but all of Saxony. Gathering a motley crew of ruffians and criminals, he tore a years-long swath through northwestern Germany, burning down villages and terrorizing the citizenry. At long last the rampage was quelled when the authorities finally captured the vengeful madman. Within weeks he was broken on the wheel in Berlin.

Reading about the latest legal machinations of the Winklevoss twins, I confess I wondered: Is it too outré to pine for the return of the wheel?

Ah, Cameron and Tyler Winklevoss, the two-headed Veruca Salt of our unbridled age. Thanks to the hit movie *The Social Network*, the essence of their gripe is now common knowledge: Young men of privilege from Greenwich, Connecticut, identical twins, are Harvard juniors in late 2002 when they team up with a classmate, Divya Narendra, to develop HarvardConnection (later incorporated as ConnectU), a university-wide social networking site. According to the Winklevosses, the three invite fellow student Mark Zuckerberg to join the team as a programmer after much of the groundwork for the project has already been laid. With access to the half-built site and all of the existing code, Zuckerberg then ducks the men's repeated efforts at communication. Ten weeks after entering an oral agreement with the founders of HarvardConnection, Zuckerberg launches a rival site, thefacebook.com. Facebook will swiftly conquer a generation and transform the concept of friendship forever. All of which will make Mark Zuckerberg very, very rich. And the Winklevosses very, very angry.

Let's face it: The Facebook story doesn't pull at the heartstrings. Harvard graduates fighting over multiples of millions isn't exactly *To Kill a Mockingbird*. But at least at the outset the Winklevosses were winning in the court of public opinion. Evidence put forth during their 2004 lawsuit strongly suggested that Zuckerberg was in breach of contract, albeit an unwritten one. And he obviously had access to HarvardConnection's source code, the same code he employed in his site. An instant message sent by Zuckerberg to a friend about the twins, later leaked to the public, didn't exactly help his case, either: "I'm going to f*** them," it said.

The initial dispute ended with a settlement in 2008. Facebook would pay the Winklevosses and Narendra $20 million, plus shares of the company, for a total reported value of $65 million. The twins had struck a blow not only for intellectual property rights but for the central code of gentlemanly conduct: A deal is a deal.

Except now they're saying it isn't. And nobody can stand these guys anymore.

Call it Greed Fatigue. After the financial shipwrecking so many have suffered over the last few years, it's hard not to cringe at the sight of two people in Hermès ties who have everything claiming they deserve more. The first time I saw a photograph of the Winklevoss twins, I actually laughed out loud. Not only are they wealthy and Ivy League–educated (and members of Harvard's uptight and exclusive Porcellian Club, which dates back to 1791), they're six-foot-five-inch granite-jawed Olympic athletes to boot. Stars of the Harvard crew team, the two competed in the

Beijing Games, then moved to Oxford, where they could be seen shearing the still waters of the Thames while pursuing their MBAs.

These are people of enormous accomplishment, and no thoughtful person would begrudge them their many hard-won gifts. But for a couple of big, talented guys with amazing hair who are so good at winning, they've proved to be remarkably small and inept at the more unfamiliar business of losing. In January 2011 the Winklevosses brought a fresh complaint before the Ninth Circuit of the U.S. Court of Appeals. Claiming securities fraud, they argued that in the original mediation, Facebook provided a misleading valuation of its shares. Their payout, say the Winklevosses, should have been four times as much as what they accepted. (Their shares are now worth at least $160 million.) A three-judge panel hearing their claims proved highly skeptical. Among other doubts, one judge pointed out that Facebook's internal assessment was only an opinion, which could have been challenged by the Winklevoss team but was not. Asked by the court how two elite scholars with first-rate counsel could even suggest they had been taken advantage of, the twins' own lawyer, Jerome Falk, replied resignedly, "I agree.

My clients were not behind the barn door when brains were given out."

They may, however, have missed the class wagon. Certainly the two seem unmoved by a spirit of temperance that, in a world cleaved by inequality, would serve them better, signifying a largeness of character to match their sinewy muscles. But who knows? Maybe temperance is a quaint notion, gone the way of prudent bankers and under-sharing. The Winklevosses have come of age at a critical moment. For decades we have blithely carried on under a banner almost patriotic in its Americanness: Excess is good, but unconscionable is best—something that may actually apply to Zuckerberg more than to the Winklevosses. We have been a nation of plaintiffs, whiners, and grabbers, and so far no economic downturn—or moral chastening that accompanies it—seems to have changed that. We celebrate the vulgarian splendor of "real" housewives on one cable channel, the overheated punditry of minority legislators on the next. We upgrade, inhale, and discard, stuck, it would appear, with all the supersized egos that have grown hale from the feeding of this particular beast. In the end, perhaps it's unfair to expect these gentlemen to exit graciously when nobody else is willing to. Mr. Kohlhase, have you met Kanye West? He's in the green room with Charlie Sheen and The Donald.

And yet, isn't our collective distaste for the Facebook affair a sign of our better instincts, a recognition of the fundamental importance of lessons we first learned on the playground? No matter where you stand on the political spectrum, you probably remember the pride you felt watching a candidate deliver a gracious concession speech. There's a feeling of safety that comes with knowing the system works, that the wheels of democracy are bolted on tight and that tomorrow—unlike in so many other countries— our more or less civil society will roll on.

It is also often our best "losers" who have the most successful second acts. Andrew Jackson lost a bitterly contested election to John Quincy Adams in 1824, but his enduring popularity allowed him to capture the presidency four years later.* Al Gore won the Nobel Prize seven years after his bruising battle with George W. Bush. Hillary Clinton was a commanding secretary of state.** Even John McCain, who grouched

*Though he will lose his spot on the $20 bill in 2020.
** Her third act will be determined in November.

his way to a near-forfeiture of his hero status in 2008, charmed supporters and detractors alike by yielding so elegantly to Barack Obama. If anyone is well situated to accept defeat and move on to greater things, it should be the fortunate "Winklevii."

On April 11, 2011, the U.S. Court of Appeals for the Ninth Circuit handed down a unanimous decision enforcing the original agreement between Facebook and ConnectU. "At some point, litigation must come to an end," the judgment stated. "That point has now been reached." Unfortunately, not really: The Winklevosses have already appealed.* They are world-class competitors, after all, spurred on no doubt by a culture that has made famous the Vince Lombardi adage "Show me a gracious loser and I'll show you a loser." Too bad they can't see that they've already won.

---

* The Winklevoss twins lost this appeal and decided not to try their luck with the Supreme Court.

Chapter 3

MANNERS

THAT'S AWKWARD!

BY ERIC BANKS

◆

THERE MAY BE NO ACCOUNTING FOR TASTE,
BUT IS A BIRTHDAY PARTY OR A PLAYDATE
THE BEST MOMENT TO INTRODUCE A FOUR-
YEAR-OLD TO THE LONG-STANDING TRADITION
OF PROVOCATIVE (EVEN PORNOGRAPHIC) ART?

When I met an old friend for lunch in New York a couple of Christmases ago, she didn't even bother to sit down before launching into a blistering description of the humiliation she'd just suffered with her kids. They'd been visiting the Maccarone gallery in Greenwich Village, she said, when they found themselves in front of an installation: a chocolate factory by the always naughty performance artist Paul McCarthy that was turning out identical little candy treats in the shape of a fat, beaming St. Nick holding a sex toy. What was that in Santa's hands? her children begged to know.

My friend was hardly a prude, and I searched in vain for a high-minded response to her reaction to this work of wicked provocation (the title of which it seems better not to mention). As it happened, I'd recently been given just such a chocolate as a friendly, um, stocking stuffer. (Thanks, Secret Santa.) Now I wondered if I should eat it privately on Christmas Eve or just tuck it away in a closet before anyone of tender sensibilities laid eyes on it.

Whatever one's response to such a spectacle may be, McCarthy had done something that's hard to do these days: offend someone who would not generally be considered a philistine. Pushing the boundaries of taste and acceptability is as old as Pompeii, where the cultural elite of the day enjoyed dining and bathing below colorful mosaics of sexual engagement. Work that skirts the edges of the pornographic or toys with the obscene has a pedigree as long as some royal families. But how to react to such work when you find it surprisingly on display at a dinner party, or on the wall of someone's house when you drop off your

four-year-old for a birthday party, has become a bit
more complicated.

THIS ISSUE IS NOT TRIVIAL TO SCOTLAND YARD.
In 2009 it pulled a 1992 Richard Prince piece—the
appropriation artist had simply reframed the original
Garry Gross photograph of a naked and underage
Brooke Shields—from the Tate Modern's "Pop Life"
exhibition. But now that collecting art has become
a national pastime for the private-equity set—
whether they live in New York, London, or Benton,
Arkansas—and a younger and more voracious class
of collectors has established itself, many are eager
to follow wherever their favorite artists lead, and
there's been no shortage of bad boy (and bad girl)
practitioners to meet the demand. Some simply play
with dicey materials or push their work just past the
edge more artfully than their peers. Admiration for
this work is not unanimous outside Scotland Yard,
either. There are those, for instance, who argue that
these artists are using the sanctity of art's mantle to
indulge in adolescent acts of transgression. There are
others who consider adolescent acts of transgression
pretty rock 'n' roll. But with collecting becoming

more commonplace, it's almost statistically inevitable that these works will raise *somebody's* eyebrows over dinner—a boss, a neighbor, the parent of your child's best friend, a prospective in-law.

One common reaction is to ignore the obvious and uncomfortable, but kids are especially ready to respond, often quite loudly. One friend calls this type of occasion the "Weiner moment," after the time a nine-year-old invited his parents' dinner companions to come to his bedroom and "inspect his Weiner"— referring to an otherwise chaste text piece that conceptual artist Lawrence Weiner had painted on his wall. The gutsier the collection, the more likely the Weiner moment. Marty Eisenberg, an executive at Bed Bath and Beyond and a voracious bellwether collector of contemporary art, was having dinner with his wife and parents a few years ago at their Scarsdale, New York, home. "We were seated around the kitchen table eating," Eisenberg says, "when my mother looked up and commented on a provocative image hanging on the wall. My daughter Suzanne, who was eight at the time, said, 'That's nothing. You should see the painting of those lesbians sucking on each other's nipples that's hanging in their bedroom'—a dead-on reference to

Nicole Eisenman's *Tunnel of Love*, which was above our dresser. We changed topics immediately."

The exchange goes both ways. The artist Walton Ford, a social satirist of sorts whose Audubon-like watercolors frequently depict animals in compromising and flagrantly sexual situations, recalled that his father was always bragging about his son's success but couldn't bring himself to show the art to the family, thanks to a nonagenarian aunt who could not be counted on to admire a ten-by-twenty-foot piece depicting an elephant with an oversize erection. "A book of my work would come out, and it would be like, 'Aw, man, I can't show this to Aunt Frances!'" Ford says. "I should have just gotten hold of a catalog and cut the pages out myself."

One dealer told me that he'd recently come to realize that the canvas he had by a prominent Manhattan artist that featured Freud on the receiving end of a stream of urine might not be the thing to have up during a playdate. "The nanny has alluded to the fact that the other nannies think we're crazy," he says. Even when kids aren't involved, many collectors adopt a better-safe-than-sorry strategy. "A few years ago I was hosting a benefit for New York senator Charles

Schumer," collector Joe Barron recalls. "And I had Piotr Uklanski's *The nazis*—a frieze of 122 portraits depicting actors (Yul Brynner, Ronald Reagan, and Charles Bronson among them) portraying various shades of Gestapo, SS officers, and Hitler Youth—hanging in the apartment. I thought I should call the senator's office to make sure he knew I was not a Nazi." In the end, the piece stayed up, Schumer and his entourage said nothing of it, and to this day no one has accused Barron of National Socialist Party membership.

Certainly one clause in the social contract involves going out of one's way not to offend one's neighbors, but what are the options when it can't be avoided? One is to chalk it up to what makes contemporary art interesting, and not worry about it too much. Nancy Magoon (and her husband, Bob, a retired ophthalmologist and onetime record-setting offshore powerboat racing champ) proudly keeps the bulk of her collection, which includes a number of envelope-pushing works (both politically and sexually) by the likes of Tracey Emin, Tim Noble and Sue Webster, and the Chapman Brothers on view in her Aspen home. "I subscribe to the Christo philosophy," she jokes. "People don't look at it until it's covered up."

Subterfuge is another time-honored, if imperfect, practice. When, in the mid-1950s, the French psychoanalyst Jacques Lacan acquired Gustave Courbet's *L'Origine du Monde*—one of the most daring masterpieces of the nineteenth century—he cunningly asked his stepbrother, Surrealist painter André Masson, to design a wooden panel to cover the canvas (which now hangs in the Musée d'Orsay). But Masson duplicated the full-frontal pose of the model in the painting, and Lacan wound up with a covering as lurid as the work it concealed. There's also the famous story of the Greek tycoon Stavros Niarchos, who did such an immaculate job of keeping Balthus's 1934 *The Guitar Lesson* cloistered in the boudoir of his Fifth Avenue mansion that this scene of sapphic sadism was long thought lost, before its hiding place was revealed in the 1990s. This is a problem not just for private collections but for gallery shows, too. When Luxembourg & Dayan recently exhibited "Made in Heaven," Jeff Koons's 1991 series of photos of coital bliss with his then-wife, the porn star Cicciolina (née Ilona Staller), the gallery was flooded with a type of visitor not often seen trolling the Upper East Side art scene after the show was featured as a must-see in a

XXX guide of things to do while visiting New York. "We had to hide the catalog," says the gallery's director, Alissa Bennett.

Sometimes tastes differ even between spouses. "When our Chapman Brothers piece was shipped," one gracious collector told me, "my husband opened up the package. He was so taken aback that he put it in the closet, and it remained there." The owner is happy to display her Schieles and Currans but admits that their example of the Chapmans' work, with its preteen nudity and freak show mutations, now resides permanently behind locked doors in their Upper East Side apartment. "For those I don't think will be totally shocked, I'll give them the key," she says. Still, the solution isn't fail-safe. "We have grandchildren who found out where the key was and liked to show it to their friends."

But who wants to keep a favorite work locked up in a closet? The financial analyst Alvin Hall decided to divest himself of an early photograph by Katy Grannan of a Botticelli-esque nude with a not-so-Renaissance-era bikini wax. Hall, who is African-American, says, "A lot of my black friends would come over and say, 'Alvin, why do you want a picture of a naked white woman hanging in your apartment?' I just saw it as a work, but a lot of these friends were bothered by it. They were intrigued by the waxing in particular." He eventually grew tired of the entreaties and, much as he loved the piece, sold it to a single-father friend with a young child. Now he wonders what the current owner tells his—and his kid's—guests.

Lubricious art can at least serve as an effective friendship filter. Defriending is one fast solution. "I give no consideration to where I put art based on guests' sensitivities," Barron says. "Anyone who has a bad reaction, I'd show them the door." Ford adds that he'd just as soon not know when somebody was offended. "I've had collectors who turn a work down because of the content—they've got kids, etc.," he says. "I tell the gallery basically not to tell me about it anymore." But maybe those collectors are missing out on more than a dirty smirk. The owner of the closeted Chapmans work is now proud of its powerful effect. "It aroused my grandchildren's curiosity, and in many ways it got them interested in art. They can relate to figurative work. That's not always the case with abstract paintings."

In the end, it may be that people aren't as easily offended as they used to be, that so many instances of highly refined pornography have inured the majority of viewers—Scotland Yard excepted—to any remaining shock value. In the Time Warner building in New York, a twelve-foot-tall male nude Botero sculpture has become a kind of kitschy tourist magnet. The statue is twice life-size, which leaves many visitors at an unfortunate eye level. Yet so many have taken the opportunity to rub the sculpture in that no longer private area that the dark bronze patina on that particular segment of the anatomy has to be regularly restored.

But sometimes it's not sex that riles up the citizenry. For the Aspen neighbors of the Magoons, what really crossed the line wasn't the dicey artwork on their walls but the Nancy Rubins sculpture made of hot water tanks and pipe fittings that they installed on their lawn. In the art world, the work is seen as a wry domestic commentary on a muscular sculptural tradition. But on a neighbor's lawn, it can be viewed as junk. "We've got a Noble and Webster with penises all over it," Nancy Magoon says. "But they made us out to be pariahs over those hot water tanks."

CONFESSIONS OF A BAG LADY

BY ALI WENTWORTH

THE PROMISE OF FREEBIES CAN
TURN EVEN THE POLITEST GUEST
INTO A MONSTER OF GREED.

My husband and I were tiptoeing out of a charity dinner in midtown Manhattan early, behind the train of a drunken socialite's Givenchy gown, when we came upon the goodie bag table. A quick primer: A goodie bag is the reward one gets for donating money to a cause and sitting through heartbreaking stories about disease, famine, or dolphins while picking at a mass-produced salad plated the day before. The swag bag holds the promise of perhaps some La Mer cream or an iPad. And opening one can be as exciting as opening the box of a forgotten Gilt.com midnight purchase, or being told the sex of the baby.

George gracefully took the shiny black bag given to him by a ginger-haired intern. Meanwhile, I lunged for the bag with the most tissue exploding out the top.

"What are you doing?" George asked, looking at me as if I had just belched loudly.

"Taking my goodie bag!" I replied.

"We don't need two, honey!"

"Well, this is mine."

"It's one per family."

I eyed the intern, hoping she'd interject on my behalf. She smiled nervously at my husband and whispered, "It's okay. She can have it."

I can have it? What did that mean, exactly? That it's my right to have it? Or that I was being déclassé, but she'd decided to throw me a bone anyway? Either way, I didn't want to be rude, so, naturally, I took the bag, which was lighter than I had hoped.

I was frosty on the car ride home. I felt like a child who has been chastised and told she can't have dessert. My husband smiled at me. "Why do you even care about a goodie bag?" he asked. I didn't know why, but I did care. I cared deeply. And then I did what I always

do with a goodie bag: I tore it open and dumped the
contents on the seat. Soap and a children's cookbook.
And a ton of tissue paper.

"What a rip!" I pouted.

"Well, what were you expecting?"

"I don't know. Diamond studs? Nikes? Free Botox?"

My husband shot me a glance. "At a benefit for nature
conservation?" The sample-size soap I received that
night is still in the bottom drawer in my bathroom, and
the obscure cookbook, ironically, was given to charity.

When we lived in D.C., George and I hosted and
frequented many book parties. The books being
celebrated were usually about political campaigns,
economic strategy, or global wars. One evening we
threw a cocktail soiree for Pete Peterson and his book
on how the Republicans and Democrats are bankrupting
America's future. Our living room was a think tank
of pundits and academics, including Walter Isaacson,
Ben Bradlee, and Alan Greenspan. I passed brie and
water crackers through tight circles of guests debating
Europe's debt burden and high borrowing costs. Wanting
to add something special to the evening, I had earlier
suggested giving out goodie bags filled with chocolate
coins and mini Monopoly sets. My husband felt the book

itself would suffice. Goodie bags are, admittedly, a rare commodity at a book party, unless you're in Los Angeles and some actress has written a workout guide. (In such cases you can score the DVD version as well as holistic massage oil and an issue of a fitness magazine.) In the end George's restraint prevailed, but I couldn't help feeling that everyone would leave our house disappointed.

I believe the brain chemical emitted upon sight of a goodie bag is the same as the one elicited by finding a Gucci sweater at Century 21 for forty-five dollars. It's all about the get. Why else would millionaires, even billionaires, some of whom own the cosmetics companies providing so much of the party circuit swag, take a bag? Let's face it: From Murdochs to movie stars, everyone makes a pit stop at the trough on the way out.

I remember, years ago, the burn I'd feel when reading certain magazines during my shift breaks as a waitress in a Mexican joint in Los Angeles. I would peruse the photos of the Golden Globes goodie bag contents each year: Tag Heuer watches, Guerlain lotions, gift certificates to Bottega Veneta, weeklong stays at European spas. All these excessive trinkets wasted on women who already had them in spades. One year Nicole Kidman and Renée Zellweger got

Victoria's Secret bras worth $5,000 each. I imagined there was some housekeeper in Pacific Palisades with diamonds sparkling underneath her Old Navy T-shirt.

The addiction to gift bags is born in kindergarten, and instead of outgrowing it, we in New York and L.A. and Dallas and any other city where parting gifts have become *de rigueur* have only fed our greed with each passing year. I still remember the birthday party circuit when I was a kid in Washington, D.C.; it was always, "What's in your goodie bag?" It was a good party only if you came home with Wacky Pack stickers, a yo-yo, washable tattoos, and a Pez dispenser. Getting that brightly colored paper bag full of plastic-and-sugar-fabricated fun made the painfully dull Duck Duck Goose and the magician who smelled like vodka all seem worthwhile.

My own children incessantly discuss what they got in their bags at various parties and what they plan to hand out at their own parties, even when they are more than six months away. Every mother I know has spent hours glued to Orientaltrading.com, trolling for bouncy balls and monkey pencils. The pressure to have the best goodie bag for five-year-olds can get as heated as the silent competition over who has the shiniest, newest luxury hybrid at school pickup.

So it's perhaps no wonder that in adulthood, maybe more than ever before, this feeling of elation at the sight of a gift bag erupts rather easily. Your inner child is awakened, and you pray you get the same color bejeweled friendship bracelet as Arianna Huffington or the same hair product that was given to George Soros. Many a socialite I know likes to say she doesn't care about swag, and yet I've seen all of them, time and again, slyly snatch a gift bag on the way out of an event. The urge is as human as it gets, but in the name of dignity we must try to squash it.

Recently, George and I attended a party at the American Museum of the Moving Image. Alec Baldwin provided the guffaws, the caterer provided the short ribs, and the museum? Yes, my friends: goodie bags! Large, shiny, pearlescent white ones certain to be filled with classic films and tooth-whitening vouchers and the same diamond-infused face cream used by Anne Hathaway. I decided to confront my addiction with elegance. I simply walked by them like a Barbizon model carrying a stack of books on her head.

The taxi pulled up in front of us, and my husband held open the door. I picked up my skirt, swiftly turned around, and darted back up the stone steps. I grabbed two.

THE HARD SELL

BY ADAM RESNICK

ONE TOO MANY FRIENDLY BUT
PERSISTENT RECOMMENDATIONS PUSHES
THE AUTHOR OVER THE EDGE.

O h, how I long for the days of thirteen television channels and only one flavor of Cheerios. Less choice meant fewer opinions, and fewer opinions meant fewer recommendations. We now live in an age of perpetual homework assignments, and I, for one, resent it.

Which is to say, if you want to get on my thorny side, just suggest that I read, watch, taste, or experience anything new. Whatever it is, I won't do it, mainly because you asked me to do it, and the more you pester me, the more I'll buck like a Chinese mule.

A dear friend of mine learned this the hard way when she informed me over a cup of coffee that I "must see" an "amazing film" by a "gifted Spanish filmmaker" called *Lovers of the Arctic Circle.*

You might not take me for the kind of person who instinctively recoils at the prospect of watching a foreign, feature-length meditation on destiny and the orbicular nature of love, but hey, I'm a complex fellow. Even such selling points as "It won two Goya Awards!" and "The names of the two main characters are palindromes!" failed to stir me. When she described the performances by the lead actors, Najwa Nimri and Fele Martínez, as "ethereal," the perpetual knot in my stomach tightened, and I muttered something like "Gee, I might have to check that out. Thanks for the tip. Ethereal. Cool."

A week or so later, as I was reaching for a bottle of Tylenol in Walgreens, I heard someone cheerily call out, "Hey, you!" Turning around, I saw my friend hiking up the aisle. I barely managed to wave hello before she was all over me like a body cast. What did I think of *Lovers of the Arctic Circle*? Wasn't it beautiful? Wasn't Nancho Novo, who played the father, brilliant? Didn't it make me want to visit Finland?

"Actually, I haven't gotten around to it yet," I said.

"Oh . . ." She looked confused. "It's just that, I mean, you said you were going to watch it."

"I think I said I'd try to watch it at some point. I've been a little—"

"I really think you'll like it, Adam."

"I know you do."

"I wouldn't recommend it if I didn't think that."

"Of course not."

There followed an awkward silence.

"I've been having pains in my intestines lately," I said, gesturing toward the Tylenol.

"I mean, for Nancho Novo's performance alone—"

I knew it was time to come clean. As politely as possible, I explained that I had no desire to see *Lovers of the Arctic Circle*, because I was absolutely certain I would hate *Lovers of the Arctic Circle*.

Her forehead took on the folds of a shar-pei. She asked me to give her a single intelligent reason why I should reject a film I knew nothing about. Gently taking her hand, I told her of my extraordinary powers of imagination, which allowed me to channel the essence of just about anything I would dislike without having to experience it. Incredulous, my friend challenged me to summarize the movie in question. A bell rang from behind the prescription counter, and I was off.

"Two strangers," I began, "converge by chance on a windswept and overtly European street where rain puddles, for no particular reason, reflect a salmon-colored light, compliments of the cinematographer whose name is Yago something-or-other." A small growl escaped my friend's lips.

"See, they're on a journey, these lost, ethereal souls played by Nubgill Newjump and Frankie Martini—"

"Najwa Nimri and Fele Martínez!"

"—and each carries a great deal of baggage, both the emotional variety and the kind you schlep around a bus station. They drift from one dimly lit interior to another, delivering long, nonsensical monologues reminiscent of Charles Manson at a parole hearing. The drama crests with the sudden recollection of a memory from Najwa's childhood, something about gathering lemons in her uncle's garden. At this, she weeps, and our yakked-out sojourners finally make love, allowing us a brief glimpse of Ms. Nimri's breasts, which are curiously salmon-colored. (Nice job, Yago! The Goya's in the mail!)

"Tragically, they will make love only nine more times during the course of the movie. Swept apart by fate and circumstance, and neglecting to swap contact info, they become lost to each other forever. Other lovers and even lengthier monologues lie ahead, but these two will always be together, humping like bunnies in the warm salmon-colored glow of their minds."

After a pause, which I interpreted as stunned admiration, my friend told me she was deeply concerned about my mental health and felt my reluctance to experience anything new was a form of emotional suicide. I responded that while there may be a shovelful of truth to that, I still had the right to mind my own business, which was exactly what I'd been doing when she first mentioned *Lovers of the Arctic Circle*.

I didn't hear from her for several weeks. Finally I reached out and expressed sadness that we were no longer communicating. I told her it felt as if Najwa and Fele were hovering above us, casting a shadow over our friendship. We both apologized, though neither of us quite knew what we were apologizing for.

One damp morning in mid-December, several months later, a small, rectangular package arrived from my friend. With a heavy sigh I unwrapped it, and there they were, glaring at me from the DVD cover. Well, Najwa was, anyway. Clearly she wasn't a fan. A quick glance at the back cover confirmed that the characters' names were indeed palindromes (Ana and Otto), thus belaboring the circularity thing.

With the New Year closing in, I'd recently begun thinking about things like change and personal growth, and something told me that being more open-minded might be connected to that stuff. "Give it a chance," an unfamiliar voice inside me whispered. I decided I would watch the film immediately, from start to finish, with a mind as wide open as the Arctic Circle itself.

But then it hit me: What if I hated it every bit as much as I feared? How could I tell my friend that I officially despised something that meant so much to her? She'd be crushed. No, better she go on believing I'm an obstinate jackass than take that risk. And what did watching a movie and learning to be more open-minded have to do with the spirit of the season? It seemed selfish, and light-years away from "goodwill to all men."

Soon I was bundled up and on my way to the Salvation Army, lugging a heavy bag full of unread books, unwatched movies, and un-listened-to CDs given to me over the years by well-meaning friends. Facedown on top of the pile was a factory-sealed copy of the Goya Award–winning film *Lovers of the Arctic Circle*. Somewhere out there was a guy just like me, rifling through piles of junk in some bargain bin. Maybe one day he'll pick up this very DVD, and the palindromic lovers will change his life. Or maybe he'll dismiss it as a jumble of half-cooked Euro-goo. Either way the discovery will be all his, free from the arm-twisting tyranny of a friendly recommendation. I just hope he gets it cheap.

ODD
ONE
IN

BY KATIE ROIPHE

TO SPICE UP A FLAVORLESS DINNER PARTY,
ADD A HANDFUL OF SINGLE PEOPLE
AND STIR CONTINUOUSLY.

Do you ever get a feeling of quiet desperation in the middle of a dinner party, as the conversation wafts from school admissions to real estate to the vacation plans someone is making to the new deck someone is building? Everyone around you seems to be throwing themselves into these safe domestic topics with zeal, banal subjects that won't threaten or surprise or inflame or challenge or, let's be honest, interest anyone, while you reach for your fourth glass of rosé. The kind of night, in other words, that you find yourself sitting over grilled swordfish and asparagus, in an extension of the conversation you were having at breakfast with your spouse. Why, you wonder miserably, did you hire a babysitter for this?

The problem here is simple: If you look around the table you will notice that there are only couples. That is what is dragging the conversation down to the safest, most innocuous level. Couples *en masse* rarely engage in electrifying talk. While it can sometimes be nice to hang out in groups of two, Noah's Ark–style, the most sublime or interesting or memorable evenings with friends occur in an uncoupled state.

In fact, the pleasant, cozy security you feel with a long-term partner at your elbow is actually anathema to a fun or exciting dinner party. It's good for a comfortable evening, the yoga pants of Saturday nights, but it is not conducive to any sort of real connection or spark or glimmer of deeper communion with the people you aren't waking up next to every morning. Whoever made the rule of not seating couples together was on the right track, but you could fruitfully go even further and sometimes invite people on their own.

I occasionally hear friends looking back with nostalgia on their college days, to the late nights when they sat outside on the grass talking intensely about

Tolstoy or love or sex or ambition or their parents, until the sky streaked with violet. In such moments those people are not really talking about the inherent boredom and narrowing preoccupations of age. They are talking about always socializing in couples. What you lose in a coupled conversation is the ranging, searching talk, the deeper, more unsettling topics, the vivid explorations of despair or failure or longing or restlessness or frustrated ambition or whatever else might be challenging to a couple's status quo.

I am not sure why this is true. It may be that married people are a good influence on each other. They inhibit each other from revealing too much, or showing weakness, or taking risks, or drinking too much, or dressing too flamboyantly, or smoking, or extending themselves too far or too intimately into the social universe. They're generally protecting a private world, policing its territories without even really meaning to.

But, as a result, coupled dinner party conversation tends to be tame. No one tells a story about losing their virginity, no one talks about meeting a man at a hotel bar the night before, no one talks about how unfulfilled they are in their work, or about existential despair in a playground. They are more likely to be discussing the cumin in the sauce, or their high-schooler's recent trip to the Galápagos.

When I got divorced I was surprised to find that two of my very close friends, who happened to be married, abruptly stopped inviting me to dinner parties. (The husband, whom I sometimes met for lunch near our offices, also abruptly stopped inviting me to lunches.) Strange as it is to imagine in the twenty-first century, I think my single energy was destabilizing to the worn dynamic of domesticity; an extra woman would create a kind of frisson of possibility, a glimpse into the swirling chaos of the outside world that would be threatening. Or maybe they would say we simply didn't have much in common anymore.

They were right, of course. I was restless with the couples topics. I was likely to bring up something someone around the table didn't like. I had stories of new encounters they didn't want to hear. I was living evidence of life on another planet that they didn't want to know about.

A recently divorced friend of mine had a compelling conversation, about her work, with a married man seated next to her at a dinner, while the man's wife glared openly from the other end of the table. They were not arranging to meet at a hotel or even flirting in any perceptible way; they were just having an animated conversation, which is, as we know, a little verboten in that context.

It may be natural to notice and maybe to mind if your significant other is too happily and deeply ensconced in conversation with someone else, but it is not fun dinner party behavior. The usual pleasant straying of a dinner party—meeting new people, striking up intimacies, floating new ideas—is not naturally a couple-oriented activity. Even if it's perfectly innocent, or mostly innocent, or innocent enough, there is an element of freedom that most couples feel a little threatened by, though they might not care to admit it. I am not even talking about flirting, though of course there is that. I am talking about being open to the world.

If you think I'm exaggerating or embellishing, go to a dinner party of all single people (or even people who have, for a few hours, left behind their spouses or significant others). The conversation will always be livelier, more interesting, more outrageous, more intimate. It will veer into dangerous territory, memorable confessions. Sudden intimacies will spring up. People will stay until two, drink too much, tell secrets.

I realize that not everyone can throw single-person dinner parties with impunity, but at the very least it is important to have some single people at a party. Now that I'm with someone myself, I have taken this lesson from my single days to heart when planning a dinner: Never invite all couples, definitely not all long-term married couples. Import some of that single, seeking energy and vitality and judiciously sprinkle it around your table. Even a few stray souls can sometimes raise the level of discourse, if they're not too busy thinking "hell is other people" while your college roommate rhapsodizes about a rented farmhouse in Provence. So the next time you're planning a party or a dinner, on the list under ice and flowers and Aperol and cilantro you should be writing "single people!"

Chapter 4

VICE

PUFF DADDY

BY TODD APPLETREE

THE JOB, THE KIDS, THE MORTGAGE:
RESPECTABLE FATHERS USED TO UNWIND
WITH A SCOTCH. BUT NOW MORE THAN
YOU MIGHT GUESS ARE LOADING PIPES
WITH MEXICAN HERB.

I am many things: a devoted husband, an adoring father of two young children, a professional photographer, a film and television director, the head of my own production company, and the president of the PTA. I'm also a daily smoker of marijuana. I don't say the last item boastfully, and yet neither do I say it with regret. Over the years marijuana has become a crucial component to both my creative output and my mental health.

I had a good (or at least thorough) model of how to be a pothead dad. My father, an anthropology professor at a prestigious Southern university, was, as were many of his colleagues and students, a regular user of marijuana. I don't think it would surprise anybody were I to reveal that a bunch of long-haired academics were smoking a ton of pot in the 1970s. In the case of my father's department—considered one of the best in the country—there was also the throwing of mad weekend-long pig roasts, the swine to be consumed in the twilight alongside vodka-spiked gazpacho ("dispatcho" they called it), followed by big, conical spliffs rolled with fine Appalachian homegrown. As a ten-year-old boy I would observe these goings-on with bright-eyed enthusiasm. A few years later, when I was a freshman in prep school, I first got high at one of the department's pig roasts, copping a joint off of my father's favorite graduate student, a guy named Stacy, whose flowing golden locks, wide-collared shirts, and flared jeans made him look like the movie-star older sibling of the Fabulous Furry Freak Brothers.

I would like to say that I became a teen pothead and then learned to modulate my weed use over the course of my early adulthood. But that would be disingenuous. It would, of course, be more reasonable and adultlike to have had that pattern, which many of my friends have had, chalking up one's stoner days to the happy indiscretions of youth. But, in fact, my toking has increased in each decade since. From time to time I've worried that there could be long-term health effects. I worried about memory loss, while my wife worried that my stoned little sperms wouldn't find their way to her waiting eggs. The jury is still out on the first concern (*What was it again?*), but on the second point there was no reason to worry. We have two healthy daughters who excel in school, get along with each other, and love their parents.

The main reasons I smoke pot are that I appreciate the way it helps me smooth the edges off life's hard knocks, and I love the way it helps me see the world. Since my father's untimely death (a heart attack when I was in high school), I have suffered occasional bouts of anxiety. Marijuana has kept my head above water. Creatively, marijuana has been a godsend as well. As a photographer, I constantly marvel at how pot unlocks a secret visual language. I see patterns in colors and shapes that I wouldn't perceive otherwise.

On the home front, I am grateful that pot can help me get down to the psychic level of my children after a tough day. I am a better, more engaged parent when I am not stressed—i.e., high. I am better attuned to what is going on in my little ones' minds and how to relate to it, whether it's devouring red velvet cupcakes or zoning out to *My Neighbor Totoro*. And God, I love eating Thai food when I'm high. Nothing beats Thai when you're stoned. There are so many things that pot makes better! Like golf.

I am not immune to concerns about how to square my habit with the norms of parenthood and society. (In fact, the byline I'm using is a pseudonym.) My mother, though she loves me unconditionally, thinks I am slightly degenerate, while my wife vacillates between amused resignation and a "when will you grow up?" peevishness. The magical-thinking part of me—and it is considerable—is desperately hoping that attitudes about marijuana will be so different ten years from now that I will be off the hook. Despite the fact that, according to the 2001–07 National Survey of Drug Use and Health, 53 percent of Americans in my age group (35–49) have smoked pot, and despite the inroads made by medical marijuana, the realistic

side of me knows that this is poppycock. Even so, I
don't have to look far to find other stoner parents. At
my daughter's preschool it is something of a tradition
among a certain set of parents to nip outside for a
toke during school social functions. Whenever I visit
Los Angeles, I often hook up with a college buddy, a
pothead dad whose expertise as an attorney leans—
happily enough—toward marijuana laws. His medical
marijuana card, prescribed by a sympathetic doctor
for "back-ache," is my ship in the night when I have to
fly out to the West Coast weedless. (I'm not so crazy
as to take my chances with the TSA at the airport.)
Although a recent study indicated that long-term pot
use beginning before the age of eighteen can shave off
a few IQ points over time, in my experience nearly
every toker I know—professional, talented, from top
schools, with great kids—seems to have IQ points
to spare.

As I did, my children will probably come to have
a deep-seated, nostalgic reaction to the smell of
marijuana smoke. But I don't want to go out of my
way to make pot smokers of them. So, as they grow,
the need for discretion increases. Both of my girls have
already inquired innocently about the contents of the

metal box that serves as my weed kit. My older child has asked me if she can play the "little blue flute"— a magnetic folding pipe—that she has seen me put to my mouth. (Gone are the fan-powered pipes that could get an entire dorm hall high in one sitting, as are the gravity bongs.) I was horrified when she said it—as far as I knew I had never smoked pot within view of her, but apparently there was that one time on vacation when I was sitting on the beach taking a presumably discreet puff. That she thought it was a musical instrument struck me as an odd testament to another of weed's great effects: music appreciation.

As an adult pot smoker, I can't help noticing how easy it is to obtain weed. Gone are the long searches for marijuana that would end in a maddening purchase of dried oregano on St. Mark's Place. Also gone are the 1-800-Weed-Deliver operations, with their elaborate logistical arrangements. These days I just pop across the street and talk to Benny, an amiable wannabe rap impresario who can always provide me with a modestly priced satchel of no-nonsense Mexican herb. And this is another thing about being a middle-aged pothead: I no longer want my weed to take me on a trip that requires hours of incapacitated staring at walls. I can't tolerate that hydroponic stuff with the THC-laden fuzz—designer weed with fanciful names, like Crystalberry or Purple Skunk Dutch Treat. Give me good old green-brown, low-key Mexican any day.

There was a time when "waking and baking" was the most exquisite beginning to any day. But now I am usually too busy with work and child ferrying to indulge in that kind of early-morning mind warp. I try to wait until evening before reaching for my little blue flute. While I would love to have a friend to smoke with, many nights find me nipping downstairs to "check on the cat" or "get my computer cord" or any other activity that might reasonably take me two minutes to accomplish, about the amount of time it takes me to load the flute and toke.

Of course, there are some things I would never do high. A PTA meeting is one of them. Suffice it to say, if ever there was one place in the world that didn't need me stoned off my ass it would be a PTA meeting, where I might actually go insane trying to negotiate the delicate egos and political subterfuges of my fellow board members. I also never smoke before the shrink, or before my trainer comes over, or behind the wheel, or before most kinds of jobs. I say most because, yes, there have been times when I've been directing a music video and have sat with the featured artist and smoked pot on set. Unfortunate new plot points have been spun from some of these sessions. And just so you know, I would never get high when writing for publication. Seriously, I would never get super-high and write about being high. Other than that, it's green skies!

ELEGANT EXPLETIVES

BY GULLY WELLS

WARNING: INAPPROPRIATE WORDS ARE FOUND
IN THIS ARTICLE—AS WELL AS GUIDANCE FOR
THEIR MOST EFFECTIVE AND STYLISH USE.

Many years ago, when Arianna Stassinopoulos
(long before her marriage to the fortunate
Mr. Huffington) had just arrived in New
York and was ascending the silken pole of American
society with the agility of a Cirque du Soleil acrobat,
she decided to give a party. For some inexplicable
reason she invited me and my husband, expat Brits,
as well as our friends Martin Amis and Christopher
Hitchens. The apartment was grand, the hors
d'oeuvres (newborn potatoes stuffed with beluga)
delicious, the champagne (Krug) intoxicating, and the

guest list glittering. It promised to be one of those magical New York evenings we used to fantasize about in dingy old London.

Except that it didn't quite turn out that way. How it all began, I can't quite recall. It is entirely possible that Christopher and Martin may have had one or two cocktails before they arrived, but what's certain is that they had been reading their favorite periodical, the utterly disgusting *Screw* magazine (owned and edited by the late, great Al Goldstein), and one memorably vulgar headline that is truly unprintable—let's just say it involved unrefined ladies frolicking in a fountain of bodily fluid produced by young men at certain moments of extreme exuberance—had struck both of them as worth repeating loudly and several times, in between outbursts of uncontrollable laughter. Unable to remain immune to their high spirits, my husband and I found ourselves joining in the merriment, until a few moments later when we were all asked, quite politely, to leave the party and, somewhat to our surprise, found ourselves standing in the rain on Park Avenue.

It was by any standard a ludicrous and not especially edifying episode. Our behavior was no doubt offensive to some people, but whenever I think back to it I can't help smiling at this strange culture clash between a band of raffish, louche Brits and the mores of the more conventional and, dare I say it, uptight inhabitants of what might be called New York society. Despite conventional wisdom—so often wrong, in my experience—there's far more of what one might call "expletive entitlement" among a certain class of Brits than there is among their equivalent in America. It may have something to do with the long-reaching, withered, but still powerful influence of Puritanism here, as opposed to the far more iconoclastic and robust Anglo-Saxon roots and habits of the English. However, now that I've lived in America for more than thirty years (my mouth as foul as ever), I often reflect on the mystery of how, when, and why some people not only get away with using certain distinctly risqué words but succeed in doing it in a way that actually ends up being charming, eloquent, amusing, and even endearing.

Though perhaps not always elegant. Sometimes expletives are just entertaining and efficacious, and this is particularly true for people in positions of power—which, by its very nature, has a way of

conferring the Bad Mouthkeeping Seal of Approval
on anything a person chooses to say. When King
George V was suffering from the disease that
eventually finished him off, his doctor politely
suggested a spell beside the sea in Bognor, to which
His Majesty succinctly replied, "Bugger Bognor."
Many presidents—Teddy Roosevelt, FDR, Truman,
Kennedy, LBJ, Clinton—have been famously free with
expletives, but Johnson probably took first prize in
that particular contest when he reputedly said, "What
Nixon has done for the U.S. is what pantyhose did
for finger fucking." And then of course there's good
old Joe Biden, overheard congratulating President
Obama on the signing of healthcare legislation with
"This is a huge fucking deal." The president didn't
look especially amused, but he had already put up
with Rahm Emanuel's filthy mouth for several years,
so I suppose he'd gotten used to it. Not that Obama
lacks a sense of humor when it comes to Emanuel's
freewheeling use of the English language. Witness the
time (on the eve of Mother's Day, at the White House
Correspondents' Dinner) when he remarked, "This is
a tough holiday for Rahm. He's not used to saying the
word *day* after *mother*."

I hesitate to bring up the C-word, but when it comes to the art of swearing elegantly, I don't think you can totally ignore class. Maybe it's the tone of voice, maybe it's the security of belonging to the upper echelons of the social pyramid, maybe it's knowing not to use that particular weapon too frequently, maybe it's just the surprise factor of a word coming from the mouth of a gentleman lunching at the Knickerbocker Club, but there it is, the effing elephant in the drawing room.

I'll never forget going to stay with an elderly and extremely waspy (in both senses of the word) lady at her Downton Abbey–like establishment in Newport and wondering how I was going to get through two whole days of struggling to keep my vocabulary in check. I needn't have bothered, because at dinner the first night my hostess complained about a recent houseguest—a writer—who had given her housekeeper one of his books when he left instead of the customary envelope of crisp bills. "A total idiot. Why on earth would she want one of his boring old books when I know for a fact she's never read one in her life? He should have left her a fucking tip instead." Right on, lady. I couldn't have put it better myself.

It goes without saying that not all swearing is equal. The problem, in my admittedly biased opinion, is not the words themselves but rather the way in which they are used. Loud, vicious, aggressive, abusive, intimidating, angry, hostile, or continual swearing is never, ever acceptable in any society. But if you know how to judge your audience, keep your voice down, have a sense of humor (don't forget to smile), and, above all, use it sparingly (as with jewelry or makeup, less is always more), you can get away with just about anything. It may seem like a paradox, but the very same words that would get you banished forever from your maiden aunt's heart, home, and, most important, will can have the power to inspire laughter and a sense of instant camaraderie with others. How about the truck driver who nearly ran me down on Madison Avenue? With the Big Mack bearing down on me, I quite naturally, in good New York style, shouted, "Fuck you," at him, to which he instantly replied, "You promise?" As a huge smile spread across his handsome features, what could I do but laugh—and melt? If he'd asked me out for a drink I would have gone.

Swearing with panache has always been associated, in my mind at least, with a willingness to take risks, and not just linguistic ones. It's rebellion against convention and having the confidence not to care what people think. To paraphrase Alice Roosevelt Longworth, who famously had a needlepoint cushion on her sofa that read "If you can't say something good about someone, sit right here by me": If you have mastered the art of cursing like an elegant sailor, you will always have a place at my goddamn dinner table.

A DYING ART

BY NINA GRISCOM

WHAT HAPPENS WHEN THE HABIT OF
MAD MEN STARTS MAKING EVERYBODY MAD?

I smoke Marlboro Reds—about a pack a day.
They're strong cigarettes, and if I'm going
to indulge I want the whole nine yards. People
walking down Madison Avenue might spot me at
night hanging out the window of an Upper East Side
apartment smoking my Reds, banished from the table
by the smoke-averse hostess. That's what happened at
a dinner party given by literary agent Lynn Nesbit:
I felt the urge, excused myself from the table, and
retreated to the powder room. And that's where I was
discovered, leaning out an open window—in black
silk Vera Wang—with a butt in my mouth. A few

people still allow smoking in their homes (my husband barely tolerates it in our own), but even in friendly quarters a request is generally followed by a theatrical display, as the hosts search for their lone ashtray, a relic from a bygone era. I have been relegated to fire escapes, sent down to the street, and given lengthy lectures about my habit by friends and family. (This happens so frequently that when *Face the Nation* host Bob Schieffer loudly condemned Herman Cain for the campaign video in which his chief of staff blows smoke directly at the camera, I felt Schieffer was yelling at me.) Sometimes in the middle of January I can be found smoking outside a French bistro, trying hard to convince everyone that winter is the ideal time to dine alfresco. Natasha Richardson once told me she chose restaurants based on which ones looked the other way when she lit up. La Goulue, her favorite, closed down in 2009.

You have to work to smoke cigarettes these days. It's a dying art, so to speak. In 2002, New York City passed the Smoke Free Air Act, making all workplaces smoke-free. In 2003 the prohibition was expanded to restaurants, bars, private clubs, theaters, public conveyances, sports arenas, malls, stores, banks, and schools. In 2011 smoking was banned from public beaches and parks. There are even smoke-free co-op buildings. And it's not just New York. In Asia almost all hotels are smoke-free. On several safaris in Africa I was out in the bush on my own, smoking among the rhinos and lions. Fellow smokers report a more *laissez-faire* approach in France, where, despite a similarly draconian ban, the habit is tolerated. Designer Lisa Fine says she lives in Paris part of the year so she can eat at restaurants with her dog and a cigarette.

We smokers remain an inventive bunch (some might say desperate). On a recent visit to a smoking cessation spa, Barbara de Kwiatkowski managed three transgressive smokes. The first involved a long walk in the cold to freedom outside the front gate, the second required a solitary foray into the woods, and the third took place in the dark on the balcony of her room, in pajamas.

It's not just the nicotine that's addictive. There's the seductive ritual of smoking itself: the allure of having a man light your cigarette, allowing a momentary flicker of sexual tension, even if he's disgusted by the habit. I like that lighting up gives me a moment to pause for thought after a tricky question from a dinner partner. I love my exquisite Dunhill lighters and the vintage crocodile cigarette case that looks so pretty in my bag, or the beautiful gold one with the sapphire bead closure, inherited from my grandmother. A friend once gave me a tiny silver receptacle for butts that fit in even the smallest clutch. She felt that if there were no evidence, perhaps it would be easier for me to sneak cigs over the course of an evening. This became a bit absurd (and I stank up a lot of lovely bags), so I went back to using any old dish on the coffee table as an ashtray.

I smoke when I write, when I eat (cigarettes always seem the perfect side dish to a great meal, the perfect complement to a glass of wine), when I walk in the woods in Millbrook enjoying nature and the clean air. (I used to appreciate the contrast. Now I appreciate the irony.) I picked up the habit when I was shipped off to school in Switzerland at age twelve. All the older girls in my dorm smoked. Back then it was a totem of glamour and sophistication, right up there with false eyelashes and push-up bras. I got hooked. When I returned to the U.S. as a teenager I stealthily smoked through my boarding school years at Miss Porter's, delighting in the danger it entailed, given the risk of expulsion. When I was a Ford model, smoking on set was nearly universal. (It was certainly encouraged when I did an ad for Barclay cigarettes.) If there is one upside to my lifelong cigarette addiction, it's the husky voice that I came to be known for—surely a side effect of tobacco. Casting agents describe my voice as "golden gravel," which has served me well on TV. At the top of that career, the head of a network told me to never stop.

I have tried to quit. Over the past thirty years I've gone cold turkey, taken Chantix (a prescription drug that made me crazy), and attempted hypnosis. I agreed to one therapy that involved being put under with a cocktail of scopolamine and sodium pentothal. I went to a famous "Russian" doctor in Boston and smoked on the way back to the airport. I have just booked a session at Canyon Ranch in the Berkshires in an effort to quit—once again.

Smokers tend to seek each other out like freak animals in the ark. (There's a new electronic cigarette that can sense other people smoking within fifty feet—maybe so you can ask them for a real one.) Friendships are built on sidewalks. Odd conversations are struck up, usually beginning with a grumbling comment about being outside to smoke. I have found myself smoking next to a stranger, only to find out that I used to date his father.

There are countless tales of inveterate smokers and their walks of shame. Writer and editor Gully Wells, author of *The House in France*,* calls herself an occasional smoker, but she still feels the need to hide the evidence—particularly from children. "I spray perfume all over the house when people are visiting," she says. Manhattan real estate broker John Glass met with a drastic situation when he stuck his head out a high window to smoke at a dinner party: "Someone on the street called the police, thinking I was on the verge of jumping." One has to wonder where President Obama—according to a recent report, now tobacco-free—used to smoke in the White House. Others find a certain amount of pleasure in openly flouting the law. "When I'm on the road," says Michael Lindsay-Hogg, cigar smoker and author of the memoir *Luck and Circumstance*, "I invoke the doctrine of Personal Space: I'm paying for this room, so I can do what I want in it. After dinner I'll have an abbreviated conversation with the friends who've paid the check,

* And of "Elegant Expletives," p. 118.

then find myself back in the hotel, sitting by the open window blowing smoke, with my traveling scented candle also at work to denoxiate the room for the spy who will come in the following morning to tidy up and, in my imagination, report the evidence to the management, who will then call Mayor Bloomberg, who will have me arrested."

THE TIPPLING POINT

BY LAWRENCE OSBORNE

◆

AN EVENING COCKTAIL WAS ONCE *DE RIGUEUR*;
NOW IT RAISES ALARMS. HAVE WE GONE TOO
FAR IN DEMONIZING DRINK?

I grew up in suburban England, in a Tudor-beamed commuter town called Haywards Heath. If you grew up in a steadfast English suburb of those years, the 1960s and seventies, you were likely steeped in booze. My parents kept a large drinks cabinet in their front room, with a folding minibar and mixers. It was fashionable at that time, long before wine was mainstream, to mix drinks in the early evening and serve them standing by the fire—gin-and-tonics with curls of shaved cucumber and full-throttled Bloody Marys. When my father came home after his commute from a market research company in London, my mother would mix him a drink before dinner, and I noticed how it relaxed the atmosphere between them. Occasionally my mother, who worked at home, would have gotten there first with a glass of Famous Grouse, her favorite scotch. A journalist and a talented radio playwright, she drank, I imagine, for inspiration, a habit that she passed on to me, without inflicting upon me a taste for that lamentable scotch.

But having spent most of my adult life in America, that easy British culture of sundowners and summer Pimm's feels distant and archaic. The disapproval of such pleasures has not yet reached the same level as the prohibition on smoking,* but it has reached the point where a sneaky, semiautomatic disdain arises in the mind—even mine—almost as a reflex. Alcohol is not going to be banned anytime soon (though who knows?), but its consumption is falling and our governments are happy about the fact. As are we, for the most part.

And so, increasingly, I feel quite awkward about enjoying my drink(s). Am I supposed to apply the obnoxious word *alcoholic*—which so damningly

* See "A Dying Art," p. 125.

evokes disease, addiction, ruin, early death—to myself, or anyone who nods off over postprandial brandies? If an alcoholic is anyone who drinks more than the American Heart Association recommends ("one to two drinks per day for men and one drink per day for women"), I am one, and you might be, too. And so were my poor, innocent parents, who would have been appalled by the word. Back then almost everyone had what we'd call today an "alcohol use disorder."

In those days alcohol hovered in the air as an independent presence: It was always there, esoteric to the children but concrete in its familiarity, not to mention accessibility. We used to play a game in the fields of Haywards Heath with the lumbering combine harvesters that toiled there in summer. The drivers were unable to see anything on the ground. We children, barely ten years old, took turns swigging from a bottle of vodka stolen from our parents. The Smirnoff tasted like fuel, like something scooped out of the bottom of an engine, but its little kick of heat at the end was addictive. We lay in the path of the harvester, hidden in the wheat, and then rolled away from the rotating blades at the very last minute—playing chicken, in other words, with heavy farm machinery. Lying there in the cool of the wheat stalks, totally out of our minds, we could hear the harvester approaching and could judge its distance aurally. Then, making a split-second decision, we rolled away as the blades whirled past.

Alcohol made this audacious foolhardiness possible. I would look up at the sky, and my mind dissipated into it as I thought, "I'll be chopped to pieces and I won't feel a thing. It'll be over in a second." But there was also the confidence that comes from intoxication, the temporary "Dutch courage" that alcohol so generously bestows. I still have that feeling when I'm drinking, say, at the bar at the St. Regis Hotel in New York: a small thrill, a quiet, discreet danger. (But be warned: If you are obviously tipsy in a New York bar these days there is an immediate scandalized atmosphere around you, a perverse disbelief. You will probably be asked to leave.)

Scientifically speaking, alcohol stimulates the receptors for the neurotransmitter dopamine. Dopamine, along with adrenaline and serotonin, is one of the oldest neurotransmitters in animal brains; it is found in most mammals and even, it is thought, in fruit flies. It is associated with pleasure, locomotion, and motivation, and it also mediates addiction through its ability to reinforce pleasure. This chemical inside us keeps us alive in a very basic way. A rare disease called familial Mediterranean fever destroys dopamine receptors in humans, producing a condition known as anhedonia: the inability to feel pleasure. One might say that teetotalers have the same disorder.

Maybe this is why sobriety feels so dull. I once went without alcohol for six weeks while trekking through Papua New Guinea, and while that experience was hardly boring, I did feel a gradual changing of the senses as the boozeless days went by. It left me with the impression of a feather slowly descending to earth. I realized that being "dry" was not for me. There is no intensification of living. While the drinker is always at the bar of life—irrepressible or stoic, doomed or melodic, chancing encounters and having adventures or lost in deep thought—the teetotaler is home in bed, snoring next to a glass of water.

I am on the side of the drinker, of course. One needs at least one drug to get one through life, and it might as well be one that offers complex taste and rich tradition. My own regime is a mixed drink at sundown followed by half a bottle of wine at dinner. Living in tropical Bangkok, as I do, I increasingly drink German white, the only thing that works with Thai food when the thermometer is stuck at ninety-seven.

I've often been tempted to write a book called *In Praise of Intoxication*, but I have the feeling that in America it would not be taken seriously and would perhaps even be an object of scorn: What about the health risks? What about the domestic abuse, the liver disease, the destruction of innocent lives, drunks on the road? What about unguarded behavior in public places?

Well, yes. But what, I would ask in return, is a perfectly safe and risk-free world, and what would it be like to live in it? Iran has no social problems associated with alcohol, and neither does Saudi Arabia. But are those alcohol-less places "risk-free" in a way that inspires confidence? I once spent a few days in Malaysia, trying to see if I could appreciate Kota, a city without a single bar. True, there was no crime or disorder. But I felt as if I were being suffocated hourly.

No, thanks. The drinker is always going to be a taker of risks, a seeker of freedom, and a ready friend. And so long as he doesn't hit the vodka before lunch, he'll live longer than teetotalers anyway.

Chapter 5

SOCIETY

THE NAME GAME

BY ERIC KONIGSBERG AND BEN RYDER HOWE

THERE IS NO ACCEPTED ETIQUETTE
WHEN IT COMES TO ENDOWING LARGE
INSTITUTIONS. BUT THERE IS PLENTY
OF OUTRAGE.

Sandy Weill, as he is known, was formerly CEO
of Citigroup, and over the last few decades
he has given so many hundreds of millions
to so many causes, especially in New York City, that
the Weill name has become virtually ineluctable.
There's Weill Cornell Medical College on the Upper
East Side, Weill Recital Hall at Carnegie Hall, the Joan
Weill Center for Dance at the Alvin Ailey American
Dance Theater, and so on. Joan Weill took a liking
to Paul Smith's College, a small trade school in the

Adirondacks, some twenty years ago, after she and her husband, who are both in their eighties, bought a country house in the area. Though nobody in their family has studied there, in 2002 they set about donating more than $10 million to help the college build a new library and student center—both of which were named for her—and raised nearly $30 million more from other donors.

In 2015 the Weills pledged their largest gift yet, $20 million, to be spent at the discretion of the administration and trustees, on whose board Joan sits—with a major condition attached: The entire college had to be renamed Joan Weill–Paul Smith's College. As it turned out, the college's founder (the son of Paul Smith, a hotelier of some renown) had stated in his will that the school he was endowing was to be "forever known" as Paul Smith's College of Arts and Sciences. *Forever* would seem to be a word without vagueness, but you know lawyers: A case can be made for anything, and once the president and trustees declared that the charter's definition of *forever* must be flexible just so that the institution could endure, many hurdles were cleared. The matter went before a judge, however, who was unsympathetic. The school's effort to redefine or simply ignore *forever* fell short, he wrote, "of showing that its name is holding the College back from being a shining success both in enrollment and in producing successful college graduates."

And with that bit of bad news, the Weills rescinded their gift. The opprobrium that followed was swift. In *Nonprofit Quarterly*, the social justice scholar Pablo Eisenberg opined that Joan Weill had "inscribed herself in stone as one of the greatest, most insensitive egos in today's philanthropic world." ("She didn't even have the humility to demand the name be changed to Paul Smith–Joan Weill's College," he added.) One online commenter suggested the Weills deserved a prize "for the grossest pseudo-philanthropic act of the year."

By this logic the only true philanthropy is anonymous, the kind that "sounds no trumpet," as Jesus says in the Sermon on the Mount. Judaism commends undercover giving as one of the highest forms of charity (below only charity that eliminates the recipient's dependence on others), and the Koran, while allowing that "if you declare your charities, they are still good," recommends that you keep them anonymous. "God is fully cognizant of everything you do."

Practical reasons for not sounding the trumpet abound as well. In the nineteenth century, John D. Rockefeller gave $80 million to found the University of Chicago and insisted his name appear nowhere on campus (although it now adorns the school chapel). Modesty? Shyness? Maybe Rockefeller just didn't want the world to know how generous he could be; his assistant once told a reporter that more than 500 solicitations a day arrived in the mail, requesting gifts ranging from $5 to $1 million.

More recently, in 2014, Gert Boyle, the chair of Columbia Sportswear, was revealed as the secret patron behind a $100 million bequest to the Oregon Health & Science University, which seemed odd, since Boyle had given significant gifts before—publicly. The unfortunate explanation: Not long before making her megagift, Boyle had been attacked inside her home by robbers, and afterward she decided to lower her profile.

It's often assumed that anonymous giving is one of those bygone values, like a taste for simple things, unsuited to the affluent of today. But anonymous giving has been unpopular for a long time. In 1912, according to an article in the *New York Times*, during a banner year for charity in the United States—nearly $250 million was given away, more than a third more than in any previous year—less than $4 million was donated anonymously. Moreover, nearly all the unnamed donations were directed to colleges and universities, such as MIT, where George Eastman, founder of Kodak and an intensely private man known to micromanage his philanthropic works, underwrote an entire new campus under the name "Mr. Smith." Only MIT's president, his secretary, and his wife knew his identity.

More recent evidence indicates that fewer than 1 percent of charitable gifts by the affluent have been made anonymously, according to Indiana University's Center on Philanthropy (which conducted its study twenty-five years ago, the last time anyone gauged this difficult-to-appraise phenomenon). Among the living, America's most famous (formerly) anonymous donor is Charles F. Feeney, a duty-free shopping magnate who in 1997 revealed that he had sold his $7.5 billion empire and was furiously giving away the proceeds. (Feeney's desire for secrecy was such that he set up the foundations responsible for disbursing his fortune in Bermuda.) Over the years, profiles of Feeney have been written extolling his unfashionable humility ("The Billionaire Who Is Trying to Go Broke"), but in terms of name recognition, he has pretty much gotten what he wanted. He's no Bill Gates.

And the truth is, being Bill Gates helps. "Anonymous donors are not ideal," says Scott Nichols, head of development at Boston University and former dean of development at Harvard Law School. "Philanthropy is a happy virus, and it spreads better if the donors are known." Nichols cites the $105 million donation that Robert W. Woodruff, president of Coca-Cola, gave to Emory University in 1979: "He gave so much money, I'm surprised the university wasn't renamed after him. The Woodruff name is all over the campus: professorships, scholarships, buildings." After Woodruff's gift, Nichols, who has written five books on fund-raising, measured the number of $1 million and $5 million gifts in the same realm. "There was a geometric jump," he says.

Also, while anonymity might get you to heaven faster and win friendly profiles, it isn't always as noble as it appears. Today's major philanthropists don't lift a finger without consulting a murderer's row of lawyers, bankers, and other consultants to calculate the less public-spirited ramifications of stashing money in a secret place, such as tax breaks and inaccessibility to an ex-spouse. "Generous people are generally quite smart," Nichols says. "They're careful. They do their homework." Still, he says, most donors don't care very much about the financial incentives of giving aggressively, but they are interested in knowing "how their gift can have the biggest impact possible." Naming—and shaming, when it comes to a donor's friends and competitors—doesn't just help; "it's something we in the development field desperately encourage them to do," Nichols says.

At some moment or another, it's difficult for any institution that relies on wealthy donors to avoid finding itself on the receiving end of its patrons' demands. Recall that Sandy Weill raised eyebrows in 2002 when it was alleged that he had helped an employee's children get into the 92nd Street Y's preschool, a coveted feeder to the city's private schools and another object of Weill largesse. The rich, after all, are used to having their way. That's part of the appeal of philanthropy. "I want to give my money away rather than have somebody take it away," Weill once told the *New York Times*.

Naming rights—or, rather, renaming rights—have become a touchy issue in these gilded times, because the size of some gifts to established institutions can rival the amounts that were required to build them in the first place. (Paul Smith's College was initially endowed with a $2.5 million donation in 1937, which would be about $42 million today.) Nearly always, the subtext is the brashness not merely of big money but of new money. In 2008 the financier Stephen Schwarzman donated $100 million to the New York Public Library's main branch, which was then named after him. A to-do erupted over whether the carved letters spelling out his name at the entrance would be larger than or the same size as those of the original benefactor families, the Astors, Tildens, and Lenoxes. (They were, indeed, smaller.) And last year, when Lincoln Center secured a $100 million gift from David Geffen by offering to rename Avery Fisher Hall after him, an additional $15 million check was required to purchase the assent of the Fisher family.

The Geffen gift has ended up causing the biggest stir on the nonprofit circuit in years. After all, it's one thing to etch new names into marble, and quite another to discreetly remove old ones. "It's just not the way we were," says Woody Brock, an economist and art collector who has donated to the Getty Museum and other institutions. "If you look at the Rockefellers or the Morgans, you would be shocked at how much they gave without most of it being named for them. The Metropolitan Museum of Art is really the Morgan Museum, you know. Paul Mellon built the National Gallery of Art, but he didn't request that it be named for him."

To look at the names of America's places of higher learning is to see our ruling class's ethnic composition during an altogether different era. Aside from Brandeis University, which was founded just after the Holocaust, how many American colleges named for Jews come to mind? Or for Asians? Or for African-Americans?

"How great would it be if someday there were colleges and universities whose names reflected a wild diversity of ethnicity of donor, that appeared to represent our population's best and most generous efforts?" says Charles Hamilton, the retired director of several prominent foundations. With regard to naming opportunities, Hamilton says, "You don't hear this discussed in philanthropic circles. You hear it couched in terms of the aggressive preoccupations of quote-unquote New Money." It's not hard to see an undercurrent of anti-Semitism in all the wincing over the Weills, Schwarzmans, and Geffens—a sense that these newcomers, all of them Jewish, don't understand their place.

But if so much discomfort arises from Jews giving buildings Jewish names, plenty of people see the value of that struggle. "To the donors, putting their name on what are sometimes referred to as traditional WASP institutions—in culture, the arts, and education—is a sign that the Jewish community has arrived," says Robert Evans, a philanthropy consultant involved primarily with Jewish charities. "In fact, it's more difficult to get Jewish donors to give multimillion-dollar gifts to Jewish institutions than to causes that have no religious or ethnic affiliation. Ray Perelman, for example, recently made a $225 million gift to Penn, but his donations to Jewish charities have been much smaller. That probably has something to do with a desire to be recognized and accepted beyond one's own people."

"It's a shame that naming rights have become so important," Hamilton says. "But ultimately it is the donors' money, and I do understand that, often, older patrons tend to be thinking about their legacy." Hamilton's own sensibility is revealed by the winking nature of the recognition his own family foundation requested in exchange for a gift to the Chamber Music Society of Lincoln Center at Alice Tully Hall. "There is a single girder named for our family, the main girder visible as you walk in on the left," he says. After a small private ceremony honoring the gift during the hall's renovation in 2008, the steel I-beam was coated in plaster. "But there's no plaque or public acknowledgment. Except for us, nobody knows it exists."

THE SWEET SMELL OF FAILURE

BY JOSEPH EPSTEIN

♦

HOW CAN THE MISFORTUNE OF OTHERS
SOMETIMES BRING SO MUCH GLEE?

W hich of the past year's* events elicited the most pleasure: 1. Newt Gingrich's ex-wife revealing that he was a wretched husband, and watching Newt squirm while answering for it during a live debate? 2. Jon Corzine being served with an additional subpoena while before Congress claiming he knew nothing about the $1.2 billion that went missing at MF Global when he was its CEO? 3. The Murdoch family circus after the phone-hacking scandal at their British newspapers? 4. The $125,000 cap placed on some Wall Street

* 2012

bonuses? 5. The revelation that Paula Deen has type
2 diabetes?* Only a saint would claim that none of
these public humiliations brought even the faintest
hint of a smile. For the rest of us, the name for that
guiltily giddy feeling is *schadenfreude*. The term is
a German construction meaning joy (*Freude*) in
another's adversity or coming to harm (*Schaden*), and
it's defined as the reaction of malicious delight when
adversity or harm besets the enviable. Round up the
usual suspects: the rich, the powerful, the beautiful.
Now add another qualification—be it hubris,
egomania, a superiority complex, or just a long history
of getting away with what they shouldn't—and there
we have the profile of our prime targets.

The past few years in the United States have
been splendid ones for schadenfreude. Economic
woes, political childishness, and celebrity worship
all provide ingredients for a boiling brew. Imagine a
police lineup into which walk some of the best-known
recipients of its dark delight: Bernie Madoff, Anthony
Weiner, Dominique Strauss-Kahn, Raj Rajaratnam,
Tiger Woods, Herman Cain, Arnold Schwarzenegger,

---

* Neither Corzine nor Murdoch faced criminal charges; the bonus cap was not re-instituted;
Paula Deen lost thirty-five pounds.

Sarah Palin, Rod Blagojevich, and a motley crew of financial titans. All acquired vast sums of money or power; all were caught going too far. How delightful, to those of us living out our modest lives, to witness, if only through the media, such ego-filled balloons getting popped, and the scalding stew of scandal, disgrace, jaw-dropping incredulity, indelible blots on reputation, even jail, that followed with such an engrossing sense of déjà vu.

Schopenhauer thought schadenfreude showed human beings at their ugliest. "To feel envy is human," he wrote. "To savor schadenfreude is devilish." The complication, of course, is that sometimes the ostensibly enviable deserve to fail. Where does a sense of justice at the failure of the wicked end and schadenfreude at witnessing the mighty fall begin? One thinks of those businessmen who are piggish in their pursuit of profit, those politicians who seem to seek out corruption, those actors and athletes who believe their gifts confer the right of arrogance before the public. When such people fail, justice, one senses, is at work. Where schadenfreude kicks in is when the failure is met with an unseemly exultation. Some people are more or less immune. No one wants to see bad things happen to, say, Meryl Streep or Eli Manning, though people love seeing Gwyneth Paltrow fall from her holy vegan pedestal, and we take unnatural delight when Tom Brady or his supermodel wife stumbles on or off the field. The old *New York Post* columnist Earl Wilson once defined gossip as "hearing something you like about someone you don't." And so it is with schadenfreude: Among the mighty, one prefers to see those fall whom one wasn't crazy about to begin with.

"The Murdoch phone hacking scandal. Has there ever been a better example of schadenfreude?" asked the *New York Times*. The paper's columnist, Joe Nocera, dissected the emotion in an op-ed. "One feature of Murdoch's career," wrote Nocera, "is that he's never played by the rules that apply to other businessmen . . . There are many people who are going to take great glee in his misery—not unlike the way his newspapers have always taken such glee in the misery of others." YouTube provided a splendid arena for it all. Mark the multiple videos, garnering hundreds of thousands of hits, of the usually elegant Mrs. Murdoch jumping out of her seat to prevent a pie from landing in her once almighty husband's face.

Most of the figures in my schadenfreude lineup
come from the world of finance and government.
At a time when the country needs all the economic
encouragement and political solidity it can get, why
are we so pleased to see more and more figures from
Wall Street and politics go down into the slush of
scandal, however it might lift our own darker spirits?
A fine period for schadenfreude might just be a
wretched one for the country. Nietzsche thought
that just about every revolution was stoked by the
sensation. "Off with their heads!" is a cry with the
shrill note of schadenfreude mixed in. The much
bruited statistic that 1 percent of the population of
the United States controls 99 percent of the country's
wealth is as righteous a goad to schadenfreude as
could be imagined. A sense that the established
court—be it the SEC or Congress—has failed
to administer the proper degree of justice allows
schadenfreude to ferment in the Colosseum of public
opinion. We wait with a certain gladiatorial glee
for that deeply satisfying moment of comeuppance.
The question for which no good answer is available
is whether schadenfreude is a sign of bad character
on the part of those of us who enjoy it or is instead

simply human nature—part of the same instinctual makeup that causes us to giggle when someone trips on the sidewalk—and thereby impossible to root out. When we see someone mightier than we divested of his dignity, stripped of his pretensions, humiliated in public, we feel comforted by having retained our own dignity, pretensions, good name. Perhaps after all, we conclude, it is just as well that we are not so rich, powerful, beautiful, talented. Schadenfreude, in this regard, is an equalizing, leveling, democratizing emotion; it flatters our self-love. Even when we know deep down that if the *New York Post* knew everything about us, we might be on the cover, too.

IS PRIVACY DEAD?

BY TIM TEEMAN

DISCRETION WAS ONCE THE MARK OF GOOD BREEDING. THE LIVES OF THE RICH ARE NOW AN OPEN BOOK, EVEN WHEN THEY ARE CONDUCTED BEHIND A GUARDED ENTRANCE. THE AUTHOR GOES IN SEARCH OF THE UN-GOOGLE-ABLE.

American philanthropist and Jackie Kennedy confidante Bunny Mellon famously believed that one's name should appear in print only three times: on the occasions of one's debut, marriage, and death. And although her name did appear in print from time to time before her death in 2014 at age 103 (when it appeared a lot), she lived a life of such cosseted privacy that in the rare instances when her name was invoked, it was with great deference. No one is sure how much money Mellon had; she inherited it from her own forebears and from her husband, Paul Mellon, whose estate was estimated at $1.4 billion. Redesigning the White House Rose Garden, which Bunny did for her friend Jackie in 1961, became the appositely stately and gracious thing she was best remembered for. When she once said "Nothing should be noticed," it was in reference to something horticultural, but it came to be the defining standard for the manner of life she both lived and valued.

Could a Bunny Mellon manage to live wealthily but discreetly in the social media age, in which the trials of the rich are put on luridly addictive display on such TV shows as *The Real Housewives of New York City* and *Rich Kids of Beverly Hills* and on the open Instagram accounts of the high priests and priestesses of the 1 percent? Could she have resisted posting the first spring bloom from her prized and supremely private Virginia garden, or tweeting when a presidential address came to us live from *her* rose garden?

"The chicest thing," Céline designer Phoebe Philo told *Vogue* last year, "is when you don't exist on Google. God, I would love to be that person!" A recent European ruling granting individuals the "right to be forgotten" by requesting the removal of links to irrelevant or incorrect information on the search engine may aid in the realization of that wish, but there is always more to be found on Yahoo.[*]

Carole Radziwill, daughter-in-law of Lee Radziwill (and one of the *Real Housewives of New York City*), says of Mellon's dictum on names appearing in print, "Now everyone's name is in print—all the time. There is Facebook and other social sites. Pictures of our lunch, our children, our awkward high school years. We couldn't go back to Mrs. Mellon's quaint idea any more than women could go back to wearing corsets."

AS RADZIWILL'S PRESENT UBIQUITY ATTESTS, EVEN for the rich and privileged there is pressure to be visible, to run the gauntlet of the paparazzi alongside celebrities. Valentino cohort Giancarlo Giammetti changed his Instagram setting from private to public last year, giving anyone with a smartphone access to the rarefied world he shares with the man he calls "the emperor": their private plane rides, their breakfast table, vacations, and birthday parties. And real estate

[*] For now, at least.

billionaire Aby Rosen kept his account open even as he became embroiled in a scandal about removing a Picasso tapestry from the Four Seasons restaurant in New York (he owns the building), sharing pictures of his family, his art collection, and even himself, bare-chested on a beach and smoking a cigar.

Bunny Mellon's memorial service provided the surest sign of the shift. Nicole Hanley Mellon and her husband, Matthew Mellon (Paul Mellon's grandnephew), Instagrammed pictures from the occasion, disseminating via social media images of an event remembering a person who valued discretion above all else. Not so the next Mellon generation. In the autumn Nicole and Matthew are launching a line of clothing called Hanley Mellon; Matthew's Instagram account is called "asliceofmellon." The *New York Times* recently profiled the couple, noting their cultivation of the Mellon brand. A woman of considerable means who prefers to keep a low profile tells one of her favorite stories about Paul Mellon's father, Andrew Mellon. When he funded the National Gallery, in Washington, D.C., he insisted his name not be used "so as to encourage others to participate in lending or giving art."

This woman says that Andrew Mellon "saw a certain strategic sense in discretion. He believed that if you put your name on something, everyone would run away from it. Matthew understands that if you lend your name to something, you might sell more clothes. So the ethos becomes a part of the business model. But the slope is slippery. *Après Facebook le déluge.*"

The author Lea Carpenter, whose grandfather was president and chairman of the DuPont company and whose mother is a du Pont family member, lives a life more closely aligned with the Bunny Mellon model. "I do believe privacy is the greatest luxury—to be truly private, to disappear off the map," she says. "Someone I admire once told me, 'Lea, the most interesting people are the people we don't know.' There is some truth to that." Carpenter, who serves as a director of her family's foundation, which distributes grants anonymously, adds, "The benefit of a private life is freedom."

Some have pursued this off-the-grid goal with particular zeal. Arthur MacArthur, son of General Douglas MacArthur, lived for years in the Mayflower building in New York under an assumed name. Then, when the building was bought by developers, he disappeared again. He was last rumored to be living in Greenwich Village, reportedly involved "in art and music." And before she died at 104, had you ever heard of Huguette Clark?* An heiress and philanthropist, Clark had a fortune of more than $300 million, which was revealed only after her death, in 2011. Clark had even been living under pseudonyms in her last years, at Beth Israel Medical Center. This ruthless cultivation of privacy is still shared by some of the very rich today. One individual who donated $30 million to the Metropolitan Opera did so anonymously. (He or she is listed in the program below the more forthcoming Mercedes Bass.)

A number of relatively private figures with public names were contacted for this piece, including Texas oil heiress and author Hyatt Bass (no response) and Kimberly Kravis, who runs a charitable foundation originally set up by her father (a polite no). Kravis is not exactly hidden away; she appears occasionally in society publications and has a public presence, but she does not participate in the social calendar or the photo ops that feature her peers. Samantha Kluge, daughter of billionaire John Kluge and, in her twenties, part of a hard-to-miss gang of socialites

* See "Maid of Millions," p. 60.

in New York, last year told an interviewer that she now lived a quieter and cleaner life (alcohol traded for juice) as mother to her five-year-old son. Kluge agreed to be interviewed for this article, then did not respond to subsequent e-mails.

SO, ARE THE ONLY CHOICES TO LIVE COMPLETELY under the radar, a little on the radar, or as an open book? A few seem to have carved out a viable modern version of privacy. Mary-Kate and Ashley Olsen are both intensely public and private; they go to public events, and the press continues to be fascinated by them, but they balance this visual ubiquity with an enigmatic profile. Their posts are dominated by press and party pictures in service of their clothing brand, the Row, itself a model of logoless discretion. There are few, if any, images that take the voyeur behind the curtain. The Olsen sisters, who have been in the spotlight since they were infants, may have figured out how to live privately with a public name and a business to promote. Even Bunny Mellon might have approved.

The brand leaders of the public/private balancing act are, obviously, the British royal family, whose members' lives are endlessly examined by the tabloids but who rarely speak publicly about them. (Princess Diana and Prince Charles, when their marriage was crumbling, were exceptions.) But look at the Duke and Duchess of Cambridge: continuously photographed and talked about—and utterly mute apart from when they're addressing their charitable and public work. They use their images in the service of the causes dear to them and to cement the image of the next generation of the royal family, as Queen Elizabeth, the world's icon of restraint, withdraws from public life.

Even Radziwill, who seems to have taken the most extreme route to privacy invasion, defends her role on *Real Housewives*. "I did the show because I thought it would be an interesting experience, and generally it has been," she says. "I think we all show parts of ourselves. It's not the whole story. No one needs to know all that."

My anonymous source continues to observe the lives of rich and privileged camera hogs wryly. "The nature of the beast has changed so radically," she says. "That said, some of the most remarkable people I know possess wealth beyond measure and don't participate in all this. One can always say 'I prefer not to' to a camera. It's not a crime to be public; it's a choice. But people seem to have forgotten that these choices link to form your reputation. The price is integrity of a tradition: the tradition of 'Do and don't tell.' It's the line Jackie Kennedy walked so skillfully."

Yet the temptation of public recognition—or maybe it's the modern compulsion to overshare—seems to snare even those with the best intentions. There's an enormous philanthropic engine driven by anonymous donors still,* my source says, "although philanthropy used to be something you simply did without making much of it, a noblesse oblige. Now it's a business. Everyone is so known. Everyone is always available."

In March, the Obama administration held a discreet, invitation-only conference for the country's next generation of philanthropists. Heirs to America's greatest family fortunes were present. The event was closed to the press, but Jamie Johnson, invited as a member of the Johnson & Johnson family, wrote a piece about it for the *New York Times*.

Whether Bunny Mellon's spiritual descendants, heirs and heiresses who cherish privacy, are blanching at the compromises made by those posing happily for the flashbulbs or secretly enjoying the colorful carousel of selfies, we'll never know. They prefer not to share.

* To a point: see "The Name Game," p. 140.

Chapter 6
FAMILY

BABY
BOOM

BY ANDREW McCARTHY

◆

WITH A THIRD CHILD ON THE WAY, THE
ACTOR AND TRAVEL WRITER GRAPPLES
WITH BECOMING A DAD AGAIN AT FIFTY.

My wife is pregnant. Few phrases speak to such an utter, irrevocable change in the trajectory of one's life. That my wife is with child is, of course, good news. It's fantastic news. And yet it is news that does not sit easily with me.

I already have two children, one by my first wife and another with my current—and currently pregnant—wife. My oldest lives with us half the time and with his mother, a few blocks away, the other half. I adore my children, naturally. My son is eleven; my daughter recently turned seven. Like most parents,

I believe my children to be more dynamic, more charming, funnier, smarter, more perceptive and sensitive, more athletic, and more beautiful than other people's children. My wife has accused me of not liking other people's children. I like them fine, I tell her, but I love my children. At this moment they still adore us. It's a lovely time of life.

The thing is, I turned fifty this year. I was fairly old getting into the child business to begin with, but now . . . My own parents were in their twenties and early thirties when they had children. These days people are waiting longer, so long that refrigeration is often involved. We're postponing the responsibilities of parenthood for careers or personal pleasures, waiting until we're ready. But are we ever ready? Much like the presidency, doesn't the job of fatherhood make the man? When I do the math, and I have, repeatedly, I will be nearing seventy—s-e-v-e-n-t-y—when my youngest child goes off to college. That is, assuming I live that long and that I can still afford college. From everything I hear, seventy is no longer seventy. At least, that's what the seventy-year-olds say. If the view from fifty is any indication, I'm sure they're right. It's just that I was looking forward to a little more time to be left with an empty nest. These newly added years of child rearing on the horizon will swallow up nearly an entire decade. And as one gets older (like, say, fifty) one realizes that time is the most valuable of commodities. It's the discovery that choices must be made, that everything is no longer going to be possible; it is a view into the void and perhaps the true sign of aging. And now, with the notion that my sixties will be spent with a teenager at home, I am left gasping as I watch pipe dreams of extended travel, time with my wife, and visions of blessed solitude go up in smoke.

I used to be grateful I'd waited so long to start a family, glad I was more emotionally mature when my kids came along. But I never imagined myself one of those fathers mistaken for Grandpa at morning drop-off. All my supposed accumulated wisdom goes out the window every time my son tortures his sister. I don't see this situation improving, as I now need longer naps than my children.

Since the day my first child was born, seasoned parents told me to enjoy it. "The time flies," they all said. And that has been my experience as well. It seems just yesterday that I sat with my son on my lap at his preschool orientation, but earlier this week I waved good-bye to him outside our apartment as he pedaled his bike into Central Park to go off to school, out into the world alone, without looking back.

The greatest, deepest joys in my life have, without doubt, been associated with my children. So why this apprehension about another? Is it just fear, the same corrosive agent that lurks beneath so many of my less noble characteristics? But fear of what? That everything won't be okay with the delivery? Or maybe it's worry that my relationship with my wife will get sliced even further, with yet another piece of her going to someone else who cries out for attention. Or how the new baby will affect the ever-evolving dynamic within the family. We already have a house filled with four divas and no chorus—can we really take on another star? There are a lot of unknowns at this point.

I take solace in the knowledge that there's still time. As I write this, we have another five months before the baby is due. My mother likes to say that the nine months give you a chance to get used to the idea—though I know I'm grasping at straws when I start quoting my mother's pliable wisdom.

In any event, we are preparing. My wife has plunged into serious and classic nesting mode. She has become urgently obsessed with finding a bigger, better home. Now. I, on the other hand, have recently been employing an equally time-honored response: denial. Just last week I was on a plane. Sitting across the aisle was a crying child in the arms of an exhausted, panicked-looking father. The man helplessly bounced the unhappy infant on his lap, but the kid just shrieked louder with each jostle. I thought, "I'm so glad I'm past that phase," all the while knowing that in less than a year I will be that exhausted, bug-eyed man. Again.

Another thing I thought was behind me was the playground. I always hated the playground. A few months ago I was struck suddenly with relief and a strange form of pride when it occurred to me that the hours spent chasing my kids under the jungle gym and pushing them on truck tires hanging from heavy chains were mostly over. The idea of zooming down the slide with my new infant on my lap fills me with exhaustion. Been there, done that.

And yet, if experience tells me anything, it's that all this hemming and hawing, all my resistance, is just "by the way," a time-filler of sorts. History promises—and I trust the future will bear this out—that the moment my new child is born, all my misplaced anxieties and selfish doubts will be swept away. Love will rush in and save the day, the way it always does when new life is welcomed. My heart will sing. I will be my best self once again.

At least, until the two a.m. feeding.

POSTSCRIPT

TWO AND A HALF YEARS LATER, MY YOUNGEST SON has me completely wrapped around the littlest of his little fingers. If only all this contorting weren't so hard on my aged, brittle spine.

ON
THE
ROCKS

BY SARAH PAYNE STUART

◆

HOW DO YOU BALANCE THE CULTURE OF
COCKTAILS AT FIVE WITH TWO KIDS IN
THE HOUSE? WITH A SOMEWHAT RADICAL
DEFINITION OF CAREFUL PARENTING.

I n my youth I was quite the daring rebel (or so I
thought), but when I became a mother I found a
thrilling comfort in obeying the rules. The experts
were my gods: Brazelton, Spock, anyone on NPR. I sent
in so many subscription postcards to *Parents* magazine,
it will probably be delivered to my tombstone. When
the experts were advising parents to have children
close in age, my husband, Charlie, and I produced two
boys within fourteen months—without wondering
what benefits the experts could possibly have had in

mind: the joys of double diapering, double teenagers, or double college tuition? We faithfully followed the PC guidelines. When our sons were naughty, they were not "bad"; they had only done a "bad thing." We somberly informed them at an early age that there was no Santa Claus, because we wanted never to lie to them. ("Let's pretend you didn't tell us!" the boys wailed in dismay.) We were terribly open-minded. Asked if he had any questions about sex, our nine-year-old said, "What's sex?" We positively reinforced the boys' good behavior, even in middle school, when it was difficult to find anything positive to reinforce. But when it came to kids and drinking, we stumbled in the dark.

The teenage years had snuck up on us. One day we were blithely discussing a possible run for student council, the next we were discussing . . . nothing. The boys took to appearing ghostlike at the dinner table, earbuds pulsing rap. An interesting combination of men's cologne and dirty socks wafted through the house on Saturday nights. Bedroom doors were slammed on a regular basis and ominously kept shut for hours. Adolescent friends, suddenly unrecognizable, stole up and down the back stairs like criminals in the night. "Who knew the kids would ever grow up?" Charlie said when the drinking began. Certainly, we had never dreamed that our fresh-faced sons, the shining lights of classrooms and teams all through elementary school, would ever grow up to be mortified by their parents, let alone to make their way through half our liquor supply in a single winter.

For I had been as misled about the reality of my children growing up as I had been about the so-called joys of natural childbirth. I had read the books and thought that, through careful parenting, my kids would grow up to be different kinds of teenagers— different from me, my brothers, and any other adolescents I'd ever known. When they were little I would sip a gin-and-tonic as I read to them in the evenings; it was my way of exposing them to a healthy amount of moderate drinking. "No, honey, that's a mommy drink," I told them when they leaned in to have a sip. I was quite smug about the efficacy of this system. The summer before the boys entered eighth and ninth grades, I allowed them the unstructured summer they had begged for, hanging out and watching TV with their friends. "You mean they're not drinking or smoking pot?" the other mothers asked in disbelief. Modestly I shook my head. It was hard not to brag. The boys had even gotten interested in cooking—so cute!—baking brownies at three a.m. Apparently I had produced extraordinary exceptions.

Then came fall, and in the space of one awful week: My elder son was discovered, not enriching himself at a Shakespeare play in Boston with his English class, as I importantly announced to the police officer on the phone, but by a city river partaking of pot, with a side of vodka; marijuana plants were found thriving in the children's bathroom; and my elder son did not call or return home from an unparented party until the next morning.

Before we could begin our moralizing, the boys began theirs, eyes bright with indignation. Months earlier they had discovered an old joint, they fumed, and did we have any idea how disillusioning it was to realize your father smoked marijuana as a grown-up? Where had they learned such lawyering? Luckily, it seemed beyond my sons' grasp to imagine their mother as a pothead. But no time to celebrate. Already the Clarence Darrows had moved on to alcohol. "And what about you and Daddy?" my younger son cried out triumphantly. "You drank and you drove." Ever since the boys had become teenagers we had been (nearly) as sober as judges. But on a recent night, as Charlie and I escaped to our weekly movie, we thought, *What harm could there be in quietly slipping two weak cocktails (under a light sweater) to drink in the car on the way to the theater?* Off we had happily driven, almost immediately spotting our younger son walking home, skateboard under his arm. "Hey!" we called out merrily. "Jump in and we'll give you a ride!"—forgetting the two gin-and-tonics with lime slices fizzing in our cup holders. Showing a derisive mercy, he agreed not to report the incident to his brother. But now the tale was blurted out.

"Drinking and smoking marijuana will obscure the real highs and lows of the teenage experience," I tried halfheartedly, drawing on repressed memories from our sons' fifth-grade DARE program, when we parents had clamped hands over our mouths as our children, one by one, solemnly pledged before 200 witnesses that they would never, in their whole lives, smoke a cigarette or have an alcoholic drink.

Parental moralizing was a failure. The books and magazines were curiously silent on the teen alcohol question. At last I found an expert—meaning it would cost me money—a shrink specializing in teenagers, though I was the one who went, not my sons. What he taught me to say was so counterintuitive, I had to read it to the boys from my notes. "Drinking, smoking, staying out all night—these are not moral issues but safety issues," I announced. "You're not allowed to drink, but if you do, drink at home," I continued, the boys looking at me in wonder. "And," I added authoritatively, before quickly sweeping out of the room, "don't steal the liquor from other parents. Steal it from us."

It was a long winter. The shrink had cautioned: Keep them safe, but don't spy on them or they'll rebel. So I didn't read my sons' journals or search their rooms (a bureau drawer filled with beer bottles was quickly shut). I greeted them on weekend nights when they arrived home at curfew (eleven-thirty) to be sure they, and any accompanying friends, were sober. Friends were then required to go home or spend the night, with their parents' permission. Then I went to bed, and sometimes slept.

The boys survived. They didn't drink and drive or get arrested or get anyone else arrested. They found passions besides alcohol to list on their college applications. Returning after his first semester, my younger son marveled at the vomitous binge drinking of other freshmen. "I'm glad I learned to drink at home," he said. "Thanks, Mom."

SAYING
NO TO
DADDY

BY PATTI DAVIS

IN TAKING TO THE STREETS, SHE WENT UP AGAINST
THE ULTIMATE ESTABLISHMENT FIGURE: PRESIDENT
RONALD REAGAN. HE ALSO HAPPENED TO BE HER
FATHER. THIRTY-ODD YEARS LATER, FAMILY AND
POLITICS REMAIN A COMBUSTIBLE MIX.

During the first term of the Reagan administration, when I was twenty-eight years old, I spoke at rallies and appeared at other demonstrations to protest the buildup of nuclear weapons.

I never went so far as to get arrested, only because, in my case, Secret Service agents would have had to accompany me into the jail cell, and that would have just ruined the whole experience. Being arrested with Martin Sheen, Jackson Browne, and Bonnie Raitt would have been cool. Add Secret Service agents to the mix? Not so much.

The difference, of course, between me and everyone else protesting the president's policies was that the president was my father. But I didn't see it as a significant difference then. I remember saying, "I have as much right to express myself as anyone else."

On its face, that's true. But it's a bit thin. Loyalty does come into play. My mother was appalled at what she saw as an attack on my father, whereas my participation in anti-nuclear events before he was elected did not stir up the same emotions.

My father, for his part, was not a man to begrudge anyone a divergent opinion; he'd have been fine if I had written some articles disagreeing with his policies, or even given interviews, as long as I was respectful and civil. But I chose stridency instead. I chose an in-your-face approach that, because of who I was, actually distracted from the issue I was trying to address. I said frequently that my protests weren't personal—I was simply against my father's politics— but of course that wasn't heard. Actions do speak louder than words, as trite as that sounds. I was a child railing against a parent, nothing more.

Decades later I would look into my father's eyes and try to reach past the murkiness of Alzheimer's with my apology, hoping that in his heart he heard me and understood. This is what I know now that I didn't know then: How you express yourself is just as important as what you are expressing. Anger is generally not a good communication tool, and a daughter publicly protesting her father's policies as he sits in the Oval Office, the elected leader of the free world, sends only one message: anger. The irony is, I was demonstrating for world peace, but I was communicating that I was at war with my father. The best thing I could have done for world peace was stay home. I'm not advocating silence or the stifling of opinions, only that a personal relationship is a weighty thing. It changes the game.

One of my deepest regrets is how I responded when my father asked—several times—if I would sit down and talk to him, listen to his side of the issue. "I already know your side," I told him. "I know where you stand." I can still hear his hurt silence on the other end of the phone.

While it is probably true that he wouldn't have said anything I hadn't heard before, he deserved to be listened to. Not just because he was president of the United States, although that matters, too, but because he was my father. He deserved the respect of being heard by his daughter. Instead I wounded him.

Another stabbing memory for me is a chant that Reverend Jesse Jackson started at the Rose Bowl, at an anti-nuclear gathering of more than 100,000 people in 1982. "Get a new president!" he shouted, and everyone followed. I was scheduled to speak moments after he left the stage, and he knew it. I should have left. I remember how sick I felt, as if everything inside me was screaming, "You shouldn't be here! Just turn and leave." But I didn't. I gave my fair-and-balanced little speech, my only-the-issue message. But all anyone who was there that day remembers is that I walked onstage after thousands of people chanted for my father to go away.

There will always be worthwhile causes on this earth, things that we need to address and to speak up about. But the manner in which we speak up isn't something to be taken lightly, especially if the issue at hand leaks into our own personal worlds. I wish now that, all those years ago, I had led with kindness, not with ideological stridency. We are, after all, remembered in the end for how we treat others.

Sometimes the political has to be tempered by the personal.

DON'T ASK, DON'T TELL

BY ANDREW SOLOMON

◆

POLITE CURIOSITY ABOUT ONE'S CHILDREN IS
NOTHING NEW. BUT WHEN YOU'RE GAY PARENTS,
YOU MUST BE PREPARED TO BE INTERROGATED.

When one meets a *femme d'un certain age* with an unusually perky figure, one does not ask her whether her bosom is real, or even whether her rhinestones are. One does not ask, upon first encountering an interracial couple, to what extent their parents were horrified by the match. One does not inquire of people who work in finance whether they have ever had a felony conviction. As Alice memorably told the Mad Hatter, "You should learn not to make personal remarks; it's very rude."

As a gay man with children, however, I am

frequently asked, "Where did you get them?"—a question I would be cautious of asking a stranger about his socks. If I deflect the inquiry, I am often then asked, "How old were they when you got them?" as though gay people mostly get children in assorted states of maturity from handbags left on church steps. Or I am asked whether I or my husband is the "real father," which would seem to suggest that the "unreal" one of us had signed on for sleepless nights and potty training entirely for social advancement.

The details of conception are a rather unusual place to begin conversation even with heterosexual couples, and call me a Victorian throwback if you must, but I prefer not to discuss the physical details of my reproductive activities with people who have not yet told me their surname. I know that our family makes some people anxious, and I'd love to assuage their discomfort. I have written about exactly where and how my husband and I got our children in the conclusion of my new book, *Far from the Tree*. I have written about it because I hope to normalize other people's interactions with gay parents and their children. For the record, I have a daughter with a college friend, and they both live in Texas; I have a son of whom I am the biological father and of whom my husband is the adoptive father; my husband is the biological father of two children who live with their lesbian mothers in Minneapolis; and the member of that lesbian couple who is the biological mother of the two children of whom my husband is the biological father was our surrogate for the pregnancy of our son, whom we conceived with a donor egg. All four children call me Daddy. The apparently innocuous question, "How many children do you have?" necessitates a monologue that I have only lately managed to reduce to this paragraph.

None of it, then, is a big secret, but I'm afraid that does not entirely mitigate the prurience of questions about whether I had to use the cup, and if so, whether I brought my own "materials" to the hospital for that purpose. This is a topic about which one would not choose to be interrogated, as I have been in the past few months alone, by a business acquaintance who had arranged a disastrous investment, by a tipsy neighbor at a protracted dinner party, by the man who was hanging the bathroom wallpaper, or by a person with obstructive hand luggage who was making conversation while a short-haul flight climbed to cruising altitude.

Reflections on my children's place in the social order are also a regular feature. I was recently at a lunch at which someone who had spent a little time with my extended family said, "Isn't it wonderful how your father accepts your children?" I admire my father's spirit of openness in general and feel fortunate to bask in his affection, but I'd prefer not to be asked, in the middle of a game of sticks with my children, to evince amazement that their grandfather loves them. I'd like them to grow up thinking that they are just as adorable as anyone else's children.

It is also of concern that so many people, upon learning that we have biological progeny, say, "Oh, but there are so many children who want good homes." I admire friends who have chosen to adopt abandoned children. My husband and his sister were adopted by wonderful parents who gave them a fantastic start in life. But I'm not entirely clear on why our choice to produce genetically linked children is subject to censure from people who have effectively made the same choice—and whom I am meeting for the first time. In keeping with the admonition from *Alice in Wonderland*, I would be wary of suggesting to such people that their child ought to get a haircut, for example, or would do well to look adults in the eye when being introduced. If elegance is refusal, etiquette is restraint.

I'm especially not keen on being asked at passport control where my son's mother is, and why she isn't traveling with us. We have the paperwork to show that my husband and I are his legal parents, but since the federal government didn't until recently recognize our marriage, the question of whether we constituted a "family" when we came through customs was open to debate—a debate several customs officers we've encountered have taken it upon themselves to adjudicate disparately. The rules are bad and vague, a situation curiously reminiscent of such loci of misery as Mao's Great Leap Forward and my fifth-grade gym class with Mr. Lombardi.

A year ago we attended an open house at the poetically named Preschool of the Arts without realizing that it was run by Lubavitch Jews. I held out my hand to the head of school and said, "Hello, my name is Andrew, and we're interested in this school for our son." She said piously, "For religious reasons I cannot shake your hand, but"—and here she smiled warmly—"I can shake your wife's hand." I tried to match her grin of radiant authority and said, "But, alas, I don't have a wife. I have a husband, and you probably can't shake his hand, either." We enrolled our son in a school run by the Presbyterian Church, an organization originally set up by Scottish Calvinists that seemed positively gleeful by contrast.

So consider, upon meeting gay parents, for instance, "What are their names?" Another tried-and-true question is "How old are they?" Also useful are "Have they started school yet?" and "Do they get along well?" I'd suggest that any question that warrants the ubiquitous preface, "I hope you don't mind my asking you this, but…" be reserved until you are better acquainted.

Here's the irony: If I didn't have children, I wouldn't really care about being asked where they come from. Just for myself, it's usually good sport to shock the bourgeoisie. But given that I do in fact have children, I'd like to shield them from growing up thinking that our family relationships constantly need to be translated from some bewildering Urdu in which we lead our domestic life. I'd like to let them be themselves, rather than asking them to mean something. We have children who are the light of our lives, and that should, really, be enough information for everyone else to get on with. At least the first three times we meet.

ALIMONY EVER AFTER

BY MICHAEL M. THOMAS

MANY AN EX-HUSBAND GOES TO GREAT
LENGTHS TO AVOID THE MULTIPLE FORMS OF
RECURRING PAYMENT REQUIRED BY DIVORCE.
THE AUTHOR EXPLAINS WHY HE WRITES ALL
SUCH CHECKS PROMPTLY AND HAPPILY.

A wise and practical man—one of the divorce
lawyers with whom much of my adult life has
been entangled—once told me, "When love
has flown, all that's left is money." I found myself
pondering this saying a few years back, when it occurred
to me how little of the money I've brushed against in
life still remains. I've fared no worse than the average
investor. True, I've been a vocational shape-shifter, but
it hasn't been all bad, financially speaking. And yet . . .

Then I realized that I was approaching a
significant anniversary. When 2011 comes to a close,
it will conclude a stretch of fifty consecutive years
(fifty!) during which, month in, month out, without
meaningful interruption, I have made some form of
payment to an estranged or ex spouse, all as specified
in a series of properly (and often expensively)
negotiated divorce or separation agreements. Through
three marriages and six children, now aged twenty-
nine to fifty-nine, the intervals and inflection points
fell in a way that never allowed a caesura.

Sometimes these payments have gone by the
name of "separate maintenance," sometimes as "child
support," "alimony," or "reimbursement for health
insurance or automobile insurance." Sometimes they
have represented mortgage payments on residences
that one or another of my estranged spouses
continued to occupy. One continual fiscal *obbligato*
has been the payment of premiums on life insurance
policies naming an ex-spouse as beneficiary. Once, I
suspended alimony payments because I thought my
obligation had ceased, but my ex-spouse's lawyer was
able to convince a judge otherwise, and back onto the
chain gang went I (with interest). Whatever name

a given series of payments has gone under has long ceased to matter to me. The outgo has been constant, relentless.

I'm not talking about the sort of hedge fund sums that big-time divorce lawyers like to leak to Page Six. But the payments I've made have significantly affected my ability to get and spend.

For example: "Didn't you have a nice early drawing by Lucian Freud?" a friend asked me some twenty years ago.

"I did," I replied. "I bought it cheap in London before anyone in this country knew who Freud was. But I had to sell it to finance yet another marital misadventure." Another time I was lunching with the actor-writer Barry Humphries, and we discovered that he was enjoying another of my post-marital exactions: a nice first-edition Evelyn Waugh that I had been forced to dispose of, along with most of my good books, to meet my separate maintenance obligations.

Pictures, books, houses, and apartments. All gone. Gone but not mourned for. Money is, after all, only money, nothing more. Possessions, at the end of the day, are only stuff. I realize that's a subversive (and possibly stupid-sounding) statement to make in our present madly materialistic era. I can hear a certain kind of reader muttering, "If this guy had better lawyers, he wouldn't be in the shape he's in. Why listen to him? What a putz!" When I was on Wall Street, we had a cute saying: "Happiness can't buy money." I have no doubt they still say it down there, slapping each other on the back as they clink single malts at a $100 a shot.

I beg to differ. At the very first moment I saw my firstborn, in 1957, I felt the beginnings of a lifelong resolution. I knew the marital record of my wife's family didn't give much cause for optimism and that my family's was no better, and I felt determined that, should there ever be a marital crisis, this boy and any siblings still to come would have as easy a time of it as I could make possible. I had then, and have had ever since, a strong conviction that young children belong with their mothers and that their lives should be disrupted as minimally as my means (relatively meager, but the only means in play) could provide. And that's exactly how I played it: once, twice, three times.

I suppose this was a reaction to my classic WASP childhood, the sort that produces "orphans with parents" and enriches generations of Manhattan psychiatrists and practitioners at the marital bar. Children were viewed as encumbrances. Money was not discussed, an omission that suggested that money somehow didn't really matter. In my own life, in practical terms, this would prove to be dangerous inferential teaching.

But on another plane it was priceless. If you're brought up not to care that much about money, it hardly ever seems worth fighting about. No divorce is ever without bitterness and finger-pointing, especially in the early going, but the one thing that keeps the animus alive is money-quarreling.

In my own post-marital existence, relations have occasionally been briefly clouded by money matters (current wives do not look kindly on payments made to previous ones), but the anger dried up almost as rapidly as the ink on the check. I have rich friends who bitch hourly twenty years after the fact about having paid what is, by their standards, a pittance in alimony, or whose ex-wives never stop badgering them about insultingly small amounts of money for this, for that. I decided to pay up and shut up; if the children's mothers would stick to their end of the deal, I would stick to mine.

Anyone who knows me will tell you I'm no angel. There are, however, occasions when someone else's interest requires that the right thing be done. I regard these as sacrifices in a good cause. Not that we ever discuss the matter, but my children seem to agree. They were not made pawns in a quarrel that really would have been about something else. They have not had to devote their adult lives to conducting diplomatic relations between parents estranged by money.

I remain friends with my exes. I take my son from Wife 3 to the annual Christmas lunch given by Wife 2 and her husband, where he can get together with his half-siblings and his niece and nephews. One son from Wife 1 (only three of my children live in the East) is often present with his spouse. Wife 3 and her boyfriend attend our Christmas Eve party, to which come one and all. I play a round or two of golf in the summer with Wife 2. I keep up with Wife 1 through our children. The six kids will always be there for one another; that's the big thing, and it's largely due to great work by their mothers and stepmothers, work that deserved to be well paid. It may mean something that the five of my children who are married are still with the person they joined at the altar. My eldest and his wife just attended their daughter's college graduation. I was there, and as proud of them for making it all this way together as I was of my granddaughter for claiming her glittering prizes. Most remarkably, I'm on friendly terms with my ex-wives' husbands, boyfriends, parents, and siblings, and even—get this!—their lawyers, one or two of whom beat me up pretty badly. It's a happy situation.

For some men, that might not fly. They'd rather have the money that happiness can't buy. I prefer the late British dandy Nubar Gulbenkian's fine paraphrase of the British writer Saki. "I've been married to wonderful women, as wives go," Gulbenkian liked to say. "And as wives go—they went!" Well, my wives went, too, and I still think they're pretty wonderful. If money had gotten in the way, I doubt I could say that.

ABOUT THE AUTHORS

HENRY ALFORD has been writing for the *New York Times* and *Vanity Fair* for more than a decade. He has written books on etiquette (*Would It Kill You to Stop Doing That?*), wisdom from the elderly (*How to Live*), and his attempts to become a working actor (*Big Kiss*), which won a Thurber Prize. He has also appeared on National Public Radio and hosted VH1's *Rock of Ages*.

TODD APPLETREE, a husband, father of two, a professional photographer, and head of his own production company, and director of mind-bending music videos, chose to write under a pseudonym.

ERIC BANKS is a former senior editor of *Artforum*, where he helped relaunch *Bookforum* in 2003, serving as its editor in chief. An expert in abstract art, he has contributed to monographs on Franz West and Christopher Wool, and to *Artists for Artists: Fifty Years of the Foundation for Contemporary Arts, Paul Chan: Selected Writings*, and *Jeff Koons: A Retrospective*. He has also written for the *Financial Times, Slate*, the *Wall Street Journal*, and *Aperture*.

KEVIN CONLEY is *Town & Country*'s arts editor. He was a staff writer and editor at the *New Yorker* for fourteen years, and has also worked at *GQ* and *Men's Vogue*.

PATTI DAVIS, the only daughter of President Ronald and Nancy Reagan, is the author of ten novels. She has contributed to the *New York Times, Newsweek,* and *Time.* She has run the "Beyond Alzheimer's" support group program at UCLA since its inception in 2011.

JOSEPH EPSTEIN was awarded a National Humanities Medal by the National Endowment for the Humanities in 2003. He has written more than twenty-two books, including the best-sellers *Snobbery* and *Friendship,* and is a contributing editor for the *Weekly Standard.*

DWIGHT GARNER is a literary critic for the *New York Times* and was the founding books editor of *Salon.* His writing has appeared in *Harper's Magazine,* the *Times Literary Supplement, Oxford American, Slate, Boston Phoenix,* and the *Village Voice.* He is the author of *Read Me: A Century of Classic American Book Advertisements.*

NINA GRISCOM, a graduate of Miss Porter's School and Barnard College, has hosted television programs on celebrity, style, and food on A&E, WABC, and the Food Network, and was a judge on *Iron Chef America*. She has also contributed to *Departures*, *Food & Wine*, *Allure*, and *Architectural Digest*, and ran an eponymous lifestyle boutique in Southampton and New York City from 2004 to 2010.

BEN RYDER HOWE is a senior editor at *Town & Country*. Prior to that, he was an editor at the *Paris Review* and the *New York Observer*. His 2011 book *My Korean Deli* is being developed by AMC.

JOE KEENAN, a screenwriter, television producer, and author, is a two-time winner of the Lambda Literary Award for Humor for his novels *Putting On the Ritz* and *My Lucky Star*; the latter also won the Thurber Prize for American Humor. In television, he has worked as an executive producer for *Frasier* and *Desperate Housewives*.

ERIC KONIGSBERG is a former *New York Times* reporter and author of *Blood Relation*, an investigation of the life and career of his Mafia hit-man great-uncle.

He has contributed to various publications, including the *New Yorker*, the *Atlantic*, and *New York*.

CHRISTINE LENNON worked as an editor at *W*, *Vogue*, and *Harper's Bazaar*, before relocating to the West Coast to begin a freelance career. She has since written for numerous publications including the *Wall Street Journal*, *Marie Claire*, *Self*, *California Style*, and *Sunset*. Her first novel, *Gainesville*, will be published early next year.

ANDREW McCARTHY, an actor and television director who rose to stardom with the 1985 hit *St. Elmo's Fire*, is an editor-at-large for *National Geographic Traveler* and the author of a memoir, *The Longest Way Home: One Man's Quest for the Courage to Settle Down*.

BOB MORRIS is the author of two memoirs: *Assisted Loving* (2008), about his and his widowed father's search for love, and *Bobby Wonderful* (2015), about coming to terms with the deaths of his parents. He is a contributor to the *New York Times*, *ELLE*, the *Southampton Review*, and others. He lives in Manhattan and on Long Island with his husband, Ira, and their dog, Zoloft.

LAWRENCE OSBORNE has written books on everything from travel and wine to autistic disorders and Islam, including *Hunters in the Dark, The Ballad of a Small Player, The Accidental Connoisseur, American Normal: The Hidden World of Asperger's Syndrome,* and *The Wet and the Dry*, which was one of the *New York Times Book Review*'s top ten books of 2013. He has contributed to *Salon, Forbes, Condé Nast Traveler, Playboy*, and the *Daily Beast*. He lives in Bangkok.

HOLLY PETERSON is a former contributing editor for *Newsweek*, editor at large for *Talk*, and Emmy-winning producer for ABC News, where she spent over a decade covering everything from global politics to trials of the century. She is the best-selling author of two novels, *The Manny* and *The Idea of Him*, and has written for *Vogue, Harper's Bazaar, Departures*, and others.

ADAM RESNICK, a comedy writer and producer, won an Emmy for his work in *Late Night with David Letterman*. In 2014, he published a memoir collection of essays, *Will Not Attend: Lively Stories of Detachment and Isolation*.

KATIE ROIPHE is the director of the Cultural Reporting and Criticism program at New York University and author of *In Praise of Messy Lives* and *The Violet Hour*. She holds a Ph.D. in English literature and has written various essays on feminism, campus rape, and politics for *Vogue*, *Harper's*, *Slate*, the *Washington Post*, and the *New York Times*.

ANDREW SOLOMON is the president of PEN American Center and a professor of clinical psychology at Columbia University. His nonfiction work, *Far from the Tree: Parents, Children and the Search for Identity*, won the 2012 National Book Critics Circle Award (and twenty other national prizes), while *The Noonday Demon: An Atlas of Depression* earned the 2001 National Book Award for Nonfiction. He is a former contributing writer for the *New York Times Magazine* and has written for the *New Yorker*, *Travel + Leisure*, and *ArtForum*.

SARAH PAYNE STUART was one of the first female editors of *The Harvard Lampoon*. She is the author of *My First Cousin, Once Removed: Money, Madness and the Family of Robert Lowell*, a *New York Times* Notable Book, and the memoir *Perfectly Miserable: Guilt, God and Real Estate in a Small Town*. Her writing has appeared in the *New Yorker* and the *New York Times Book Review.*

ALEXANDRA STYRON is the author of the novel *All the Finest Girls*, and a memoir, *Reading My Father*, about life with her father, the writer William Styron. She has written for the *Financial Times*, the *New Yorker*, the *Wall Street Journal*, and *Vanity Fair*, and currently teaches memoir writing at Hunter College.

TIM TEEMAN is an editor at the *Daily Beast*. He spent fourteen years at the *Times* in London before moving to New York City to work as its U.S. correspondent. His first book, *In Bed with Gore Vidal: Hustlers, Hollywood, and the Private World of an American Master*, was nominated for a 2014 Lambda Literary Award.

MICHAEL M. THOMAS was a curator at the Metropolitan Museum of Art and a partner at Lehman Brothers prior to becoming a writer in 1978. He is now the best-selling author of nine novels, including *Fixers*, which was published in January. He has contributed to the *New York Times*, the *Washington Post*, and the *Wall Street Journal*, and was a columnist for the *New York Observer*.

GULLY WELLS, the daughter of American journalist Dee Wells and stepdaughter of British philosopher A. J. "Freddie" Ayer, spent her childhood in the sixties among London's intellectual elite, which she documented in her 2011 memoir, *The House in France.* She is a contributing editor to *Condé Nast Traveler.*

ALI WENTWORTH is an actress, comedian, producer, and author of *Ali in Wonderland: And Other Tall Tales, Happily Ali After: And Other Fairly True Tales,* and *The WASP Cookbook.* Her mother, Muffie Brandon Cabot, was Nancy Reagan's White House social secretary, and her father, Eric Wentworth, was a reporter for the *Washington Post.* She is married to George Stephanopoulos, ABC News' chief anchor and former political adviser to the Clinton administration.

ALEXANDRA WOLFE is a staff reporter for the *Wall Street Journal* and author of the weekly column "Weekend Confidential." She is a former staff reporter for the *New York Observer* and has written for *Bloomberg Businessweek, Travel + Leisure, Departures,* and *Vanity Fair.* Her first novel, *The Valley of the Gods: A Silicon Valley Story,* will be released early next year.

INDEX